THE OAKWOOD PRESS
The First 80 Years

1931 - 2011
A Collector's Guide

by
Terence A. Mullarkey

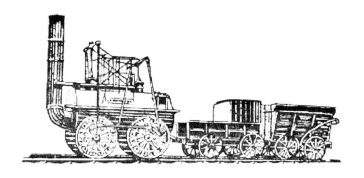

THE OAKWOOD PRESS

© Oakwood Press & Terence A. Mullarkey 2012

British Library Cataloguing in Publication Data
A Record for this book is available from the British Library
ISBN 978 0 85361 719 8

Typeset by Oakwood Graphics.
Repro by PKmediaworks, Cranborne, Dorset.
Printed by Information Press Ltd, Eynsham, Oxford.

Oakwood Press proprietors,
above left, R.W. Kidner (1930s-1984), *above right*, Jane Kennedy (1984-to the present day).

Published by The Oakwood Press (Usk), P.O. Box 13, Usk, Mon., NP15 1YS.
E-mail: sales@oakwoodpress.co.uk
Website: www.oakwoodpress.co.uk
Facebook: Oakwood Press Books and Visuals

Contents

Introduction

The main purpose of this guide, as well as briefly telling the story of Oakwood Press, is to detail and illustrate fully all of the books and associated items that Oakwood have published over the past 80 years.

As a long-standing enthusiastic reader of railway books, over the years I acquired a large collection of Oakwood Press titles, which I particularly enjoy reading. But tracking down exactly which titles I still needed was proving difficult, so in 1995 I contacted Oakwood Press to see if there was a complete list of all its titles, but was advised that a full list did not exist. A list of known titles was available, but it was incomplete.

So with the knowledge I had already gained and a further 16 years of steady research, with many head scratching moments, including tracking down some elusive titles all over the world, I hope this book now fills that gap and will be of interest to all serious transport enthusiasts. I am sure there will be the odd error or omission in what turned out to be a very complex story, with much conflicting data. If anyone has any further information I would be most interested in details (with evidence) via the publishers or Facebook (*see page 2*).

Oakwood has certainly become a legend in publishing transport history and is the oldest specialist British transport publisher of its type still extant. Oakwood titles have now been published for 80 years and continue to appeal to connoisseurs of transport publishing and long may they do so.

The publisher's address on individual Oakwood Press books can sometimes help date the edition. These are Oakwood's addresses over the years.

1931-1939	19 The Drive, Sidcup, Kent.
1940-1945	No books published – war service.
1946-1947	30 White Horse Hill, Chislehurst, Kent.
1947-1953	Tanglewood, South Godstone, Surrey.
1954-1956	During this period moved into temporary accommodation.
1957-1961	Bucklands, Tandridge Lane, Lingfield, Surrey.
1961-1974	Tandridge Lane, Lingfield, Surrey.
1975	Order from Element Books, Old Brewery, Tisbury, Salisbury.
1976-1980	Old School House, Tarrant Hinton, near Blandford, Dorset.
1981-1984	Tarrant Cottage, Great Hinton, Trowbridge, Wilts.
	Order from Element Books, Old Brewery, Tisbury,
	Salisbury - distributors.
1984	Change of ownership.
1984-1997	P.O. Box 122, Headington, Oxford.
1998-to date	P.O. Box 13, Usk, Mon., NP15 1YS.

As with most successful undertakings there are dedicated people behind them, Roger Wakely Kidner was certainly the driving force behind Oakwood in the early days and Jane Kennedy has more recently very successfully carried on his legacy. Regrettably I never met Roger, but Jane has been very helpful in supplying information and encouraging my efforts.

I present this guide with fond memories of all those various little railways which feature in so many Oakwood books and also in memory of Roger 'R.W.' Kidner who sadly passed away 14th September, 2007, aged 93 - a real pioneer in railway publishing and writer of over 50 Oakwood books.

Historical Summary

The publishing of the small, quarterly railway magazine *Locomotion*, under 'The Four Os Publishing' name by R. Michael Robbins and Roger W. Kidner in Sidcup, Kent during March 1931, marked the start of the Oakwood story. Michael edited the first editions but Roger took over as editor in September 1933. By September 1934 progress meant much improved production methods, with printing taking over from the original duplicated sheets.

Meanwhile during 1935 a small booklet, *A Railway Library - A List of Railway Books*, was published still using the name ' Four Os Publishing Co.' starting the move into book publishing. By 1936 with the appearance of the first of the popular Light Railway Handbooks, *The Lynton and Barnstaple Railway* (since much reprinted), 'Oakwood Press' became the chosen publishing title. The name Oakwood Press was born as the manuscript was virtually on its way to the printer, and with Roger away at the time, Robbins and the author, Leslie Catchpole, came up with the name as an amalgam of 'The Oaks' and 'Southwood', the names of the houses that Roger was moving from and to.

September 1937 saw the publishing of *The North London Railway* (OL1) starting the now familiar Oakwood Library of Railway History series. In 1938 a pioneering trainspotters' aid was published, *How to Recognise Southern Railway Locomotives*. Only a few other titles appeared before the war interrupted things in 1939 and all publishing was suspended. From 1940 to 1945 both Roger W. Kidner and R. Michael Robbins were in the forces on war service and no books were published during this period.

By 1946 Oakwood was publishing again, now from Chislehurst, Kent. Oakwood moved to South Godstone, Surrey in 1947 and R. Michael Robbins left Oakwood about this time to pursue a career with London Transport, leaving R.W. Kidner at the helm. Despite this Roger's involvement in Oakwood would remain part time until around 1972 with his wife Beryl taking an everyday rôle.

With the decision, driven by paper rationing legislation, not to revive the *Locomotion* magazine and print occasional Locomotion Papers instead, 1947 saw the printing of the first Locomotion Papers (LP1), *The Alford and Sutton Tramway*. LP1 was also subtitled '*Locomotion* Vol. X1 No. 35 July 1947', following on the sequence from the last *Locomotion* magazine No. 34.

Interestingly Oakwood books also soon became known in other countries and *History of Motorized Vehicles: Mechanical Traction and Travel 1769 to 1946* by R.W. Kidner was published in the USA during 1949 by Floyd Clymer of Los Angeles.

The year 1949 also saw J.I.C. Boyd's *Narrow Gauge Rails to Portmadoc* published, starting an important series of narrow gauge railway titles. During the 1950s along with an increase of interest in railway books, Oakwood's range of titles gradually expanded along with its reputation as specialized transport publishers, especially railways, and by the 1960s also included a canal series.

Little known to many, along with the transport titles during the 1950s and 1960s, there were also other small series of specialist books on such diverse subjects as market research and gramophone records. These were published right up to the 1970s.

During 1957 Oakwood had moved to Lingfield, Surrey and by 1975 to Tarrant Hinton, near Blandford, Dorset, then in 1981 to Great Hinton, Trowbridge, Wilts. With Roger Kidner's enthusiasm and the assistance of his wife Beryl, new titles continued apace until in 1984 at the age of 70 Roger decided it was time to take a back seat and he sold Oakwood Press to Jane Kennedy.

Jane Kennedy formerly of Oxford Publishing Company took over Oakwood in October 1984 and soon enthusiastically expanded the range of titles, subtly adding her own style into Oakwood, whilst still maintaining the main theme, starting with LP154 in 1985. Since then many new titles have been published expanding the existing series as well as many reprints of popular earlier titles. New series have also appeared, the Portfolio series in 1985, the Portrait series in 1992 and the Reminiscence series in 1994. Moving with the times a specialist range of videos were also introduced, starting in 1993, these being the products of Oakwood Video Library, an associated company. A detailed annual catalogue also appeared in 1988 and collectors' bookmarks followed in 1989. Roger continued to take an interest in Oakwood on a consultancy basis, always happy to offer helpful advice.

Jane Kennedy operated Oakwood from Oxford, until moving to Usk, Monmouthshire, in 1998. The new millennium saw the Oakwood Press range continuing to expand with many more specialist transport book titles being published and a range of DVDs following on from the videos. A website was also launched in 2000. Sadly Roger Kidner passed away on 14th September, 2007 at the age of 93, ending an association with Oakwood that had lasted over 75 years, a truly remarkable achievement. He left a lasting testament of his dedication to specialist transport publishing that we can all enjoy for years to come and with already over 25 years managing the business Jane Kennedy ably carries the story of Oakwood into the future.

The appearance of Oakwood books over the years

Most of the early titles were published in very small numbers, as stapled paperbacks, with very plain simple line-drawn illustrated covers. The books were generally all of a similar size (with a few variations) but mainly around A5 format, which is still the standard well known size of titles today. Thread-sewn binding was also employed for a while but later reprints and new issues were usually stapled. Most covers gradually benefited from better card and photographic illustrations, colour was also introduced. A few of the early titles had hardback binding, some were also published in both soft back and cloth bound (hardback) editions, and a very small number were bound with boards with quarter cloth. Latterly hardback editions, complete with dust jackets, were mainly for the more bulky titles, the majority have always been paperback. From 1985 to 1998 most titles were square-backed bound with Linson covers, and then, more recently, with all-colour glossy card laminated covers. In many ways the appearance of Oakwood books reflects the general changes in book production over the last 80 years.

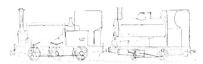

Delightful simple early line drawings, 1938

Later line drawing, 1965

Listing Oakwoods

Section One of this book acts as an introduction. It is then followed by books A1 to X99. Each series of Oakwood books has a letter(s) and number reference e.g. LP1, OL1 etc. The listing is in alphabetical/numerical order, with an illustration of each edition and reprints following each section. There is also a full title alphabetical index on pages 92 to 98 to aid finding reference details of individual titles.

Oakwood did not publish all editions of a few titles; to give complete details and explain seemingly missing books, where this is known, a note to that effect is included in the title listing, e.g. C8 (1979 First Edition not Oakwood). Also a limited number of titles changed with new editions, this being identified by some reference to the change in brackets after the original title, e.g. LP8 *Traction Engine 1842-1936* ('1842-1936' only on 1966 edition). Sometimes new editions were given a new title and new reference, these are also referred to in brackets after the title, e.g. LP12 *Development of the Railcar* (NB: updated version of A21). Any useful miscellaneous information is also recorded in this way such as: LP9 *History of the Steam Tram* (based on a 1937 Paper). Appendices detail Oakwood books on gramophone records and market research, postcards, videos, DVDs, tapes, catalogues, bookmarks.

Oakwood titles are very collectable, and with a little searching even some of the earlier titles are available second-hand at quite reasonable prices. You can, however, expect to pay premium prices for some of the rarer out of print titles in good condition and some can be quite difficult to come across. New titles and reprints do of course appear regularly to add to your collection.

With many reprints and new editions of some titles, knowing for sure which copy you are looking at is not always as straightforward as it seems and careful scrutiny is sometimes required. Appropriate information was not always recorded in each update (especially in the early years), sometimes simply just repeating information from the previous print and repeating the cover design as well, making it very difficult.

Prices printed on the book can be a big clue: if what seems to be the same edition, but has a higher price, it is obviously a later printing (ignoring of course the extra stick-on price tickets that were applied when inflation was rife during the 1970s and 1980s). Where the cover design changed for a new edition this is easily recognized, but details inside don't always reflect this; sometimes there are clues within the book like dated late amendments or new introduction notes. A lot of books have a list of titles on the back cover, this can also help date editions, as can the address at the time of publishing. Another example of subtle differences - on the front covers of LP57 to LP79 the first edition has 'Locomotion Papers' printed in white, later editions had normal black print. I was amazed how many different editions I found when I carefully studied many titles. No official complete record of all the Oakwood books published was ever maintained, so what follows attempts to remedy this.

Locomotion Magazine, Four Os and America

The Locomotion Magazine

The publishing of the small, simply-produced quarterly railway magazine *Locomotion* in Sidcup, Kent during March 1931 marked the start of the Oakwood story. Schoolfriends R. Michael Robbins and Roger W. Kidner were involved in producing the magazine, early copies were simply typed and duplicated until printing took over as the magazine progressed.

Each edition had a thin card cover with a varying simple line drawing on the front. Priced at 6*d*. to start with, the price rose to 1*s*. from December 1938 when there was also an increase in pages from 16 to 24. With the outbreak of World War II publishing was suspended in September 1939 and only 34 editions of *Locomotion* were ever published.

The magazine's aim was to try to make an important addition to railway history, as indeed Oakwood Press have in their own unique way ever since. Articles covered a wide range of subjects including: railway tickets, Whale locomotives of the LNWR, notes on the naming of locomotives, table of early locomotive builders 1825-1864, Cleobury Mortimer & Ditton Priors Light Railway, Castlecary, the race to Edinburgh, the Midland Railway's West Riding lines, Rhondda & Swansea Bay Railway locomotives, to name but a few, *Locomotion* was only produced in small numbers so copies are quite difficult to find and are rarely offered for sale.

Four Os Publishing

In 1935 an interesting small booklet *A Railway Library - A List of Railway Books* by Canon R.B. Fellows appeared, printed and published by the Four Os Publishing Co. publishers of the *Locomotion* magazine, R.M. Robbins & R.W. Kidner, starting the Oakwood Press story. The Four O's name referred to the four Os in 'Locomotion'.

Oakwood in America

Oakwood books soon became known in other countries and *History of Motorized Vehicles: Mechanical Traction and Travel 1769 to 1946* by R.W. Kidner was published in the USA in 1949 by Floyd Clymer of Los Angeles. Encompassing three volumes in one book, originally these had been published in England by Oakwood as *The Early History of the Motor Car 1769-1897*, *The Development of Road Motors 1898-1946*, and *The Steam Lorry 1896-1939*. Comprising 160 pages with many illustrations it was priced at two dollars, and can still be found second-hand today in the USA.

'A' Series

Oakwood do not actually use the 'A' prefix (starting with B) but to aid identity 'A' is used in this guide for various titles that Oakwood haven't given a letter prefix to, including 'The Light Railway Handbook' series, 'The Short History of Mechanical Traction and Travel' series and various other unusual miscellaneous titles, including some non-transport titles.

Light Railway Handbooks

This popular and much reprinted series with its somewhat complicated history, with many reprints, re-titling and revamping of various editions was a real challenge to decipher, but equally a delight. The early editions in particular with their characteristic thin card covers containing perhaps just 12, 16 or 20 stapled-in pages give a charming insight into their subject with their delightful simple line drawings, all leaving you wanting to find out more about the enchanting lines covered.

Note that A1A is the original A1 title expanded with the addition of the original A4 Handbook, so is actually the first edition in this format. A4A is a combined edition of A5 and A6. Also title A9 combines various editions of the handbooks depending on the year of printing.

A1	Light Railway Handbook No. 1 Colonel Stephens Railways	R.W. Kidner
A1A*	Light Railway Handbook No. 1 Standard Gauge Light Railways	R.W. Kidner
A2	Light Railway Handbook No. 2 Narrow Gauge Railways of (North) Wales	R.W. Kidner
A3	Light Railway Handbook No. 3 English Narrow Gauge Railways	R.W. Kidner
A4	Light Railway Handbook No. 4 Standard Gauge Light Railways	R.W. Kidner
A4A	Light Railway Handbook No. 4 Narrow Gauge Railways of Ireland	R.W. Kidner
A5	Light Railway Handbook No. 5 3 ft Gauge Railways of Northern Ireland	R.W. Kidner
A6	Light Railway Handbook No. 6 Light Railways of Eire, IOM & CI	R.W. Kidner
A7	Light Railway Handbook No. 7 Mineral Railways	R.W. Kidner
A8	Light Railway Handbook No. 8 (Light and) Narrow Gauge Locomotives	R.W. Kidner
A9	Light Railway Handbook British Light Railways (combinations of above)	R.W. Kidner
A9A	Light Railways Handbook Appendices A & B	R.W. Kidner
A10	Light Railways of Britain	R.W. Kidner
A11	Narrow Gauge Railways (combination of A2, A3, A4A)	R.W. Kidner

A Short History of Mechanical Traction and Travel

A12	Early History of the Motor Car 1769-1897 (Part 1)	R.W. Kidner
A13	Development of Road Motors 1898-1946 (Part 2)	R.W. Kidner
A14	Early History of the Railway Locomotive 1804-1879 (Part 3)	R.W. Kidner
A15	Development of the Railway Locomotive 1880-1946 (Part 4)	R.W. Kidner
A16	Railway Carriage 1825-1946 (Part 5)	R.W. Kidner
A17	Multiple Unit Trains, Railmotors and Tramcars 1829-1947 (Part 6)	R.W. Kidner
A18	Short History of Mechanical Traction and Travel Vol.1 Road (Parts 1, 2)	R.W. Kidner
A19	Short History of Mechanical Traction and Travel Vol.2 Rail (Parts 3-6)	R.W. Kidner

* LP129 is an expanded and revised version of A1A.

Miscellaneous Titles

This small diverse selection of books for various reasons didn't receive any alphabetical or numerical references by Oakwood, and are grouped together just for that reason.

A20	*Skipper Looks Back*	F.W. Dean
A21	*How to Recognise Southern Railway Locomotives*	R.W. Kidner
A22	*Railcar 1847-1939 (NB: LP12)*	R.W. Kidner
A23	*Steam Lorry Album* (Repro. of photographs from early technical journals)	Unattributed
A24	*Shaftesbury and its Abbey*	L. Sydenham
A25	*Layman's Diagnosis of the Human Situation*	J.A. Hathom
A26	*General Motor Bus Album* (Photographs of the vehicles from 1904 to 1932)	Unattributed
A27	*History of Bradford Trolley Buses 1911-1960*	H. Brearley
A28*	*English Farm Wagon Origins & Structure* (1972/7/81 eds. not Oakwood)	J.G. Jenkins
A29	*Calshot RAF Railway*	F.W. Cooper
A30	*Contractors Locomotive Album* (35 photographs)	R.W. Kidner
A31*	*West Country Friendly Societies*	M.D. Fuller
A32†	*Our History The First Fifty Years 1910-1960 by Oxfordshire Guides*	Oxfordshire Guides

A1 - 1936 - 1st   A1 - 1937 - 2nd   A1 - 1946 - 2nd rp   A1 - 1948 - 3rd

A1A - 1953 - 4th   A1A - 1965 - 5th   A1A - 1971 - 6th

* Published by Oakwood for the Museum of English Rural Life, University of Reading.
† Published by Oxfordshire Guides - Distributed by Oakwood.

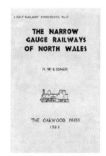

A2 - 1936 - 1st

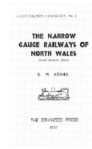

A2 - 1937 - 2nd

A2 - 1947 - 3rd

A2 - 1956 - 4th

A2 - c.1960 - 5th

A2 - 1964 - 6th

A2 - 1966 - 7th

A2 - 1969 - 8th

A2 - 1970 - 9th

A2 - 1972 - 10th

A3 - 1937 (Mar.) - 1st

A3 - 1937 (Nov.) - 2nd

A3 - 1943 - 2nd rp

A3 - 1947 - 3rd

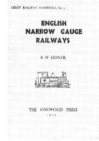

A3 - c.1958 - 4th

A3 - 1964 - 5th

A3 - 1970 - 6th   A4 - 1937 - 1st   A4 - 1947 - 2nd   A4A - 1958 - 3rd

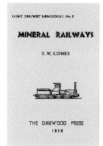

A4A - 1965 - 4th   A4A - 1971 - 5th   A5 - 1937 - 1st   A5 - 1950 - 2nd

A6 - 1938 - 1st   A6 - 1949 - 2nd   A7 - 1938 - 1st   A7 - 1946 - 2nd

A7 - 1954 - 3rd   A7 - 1961 - 4th   A7 - 1967 - 5th   A8 - 1939 - 1st

A8 - 1949 - 2nd

A8 - 1960 - 3rd

A9 - 1938 - 1st

A9 - 1950* - 2nd 12s.

Notes

* Updated with 1.12.1951 loose sheet.

† Reprints with appendices (A9A) and 1.4.1952 updates bound in, with and without 1950 on the front.

A9 - 1950† - 2nd 13s. 6d.

Unable to trace a copy of this edition for illustration

A9 - c.1955 - 3rd

A9 - c.1961 - 4th

A9 - 1965 - 5th

A9 - 1971 - 6th

A9A - 1952

A10 - 1947

A11 - c.1961

A12 - 1946

A13 - 1946

A14 - 1946

A15 - 1946

A16 - 1946

A17 - 1947

A18 - 1947

A19 - 1947

A20 - 1937

A21 - 1938

A22 - 1939

A23 - c.1953

A24 - 1959

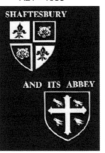

A24 - 1978

A LAYMAN'S DIAGNOSIS
OF THE
HUMAN SITUATION

by
J. A. HAWTHORN

THE OAKWOOD PRESS

A25 - 1960

A26 - 1960 - 3s.

A26 - 196? - 3s. 6d.

A27 - 1960

A28 - 1961

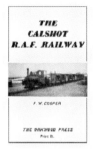   

A29 - 1963   A30 - 1964   A31 - 1964   A32 - 1999

The Oakwood Press

R. W. Kidner
B. Kidner

Tarrant Cottage, Great Hinton
TROWBRIDGE, Wilts. BA14 6BY

Tel. 0380 870 621

LIGHT RAILWAY HANDBOOKS

1. The Colonel Stephens Railways Last edn 3rd 1949 then in with 4
2. Narrow Gauge Railways of Wales Last edn 10th 1972
3. English Narrow Gauge Railways last edn 1970
4. Standard Gauge Light Railways Last end 6th 1971
5. N G Railways of N.Ireland Last edn 2nd 1950, then in with 6
6. Light Rlys of Eire Last edn 2nd. 1949 then with 5 as 'N G Rly
                                    of Ireland' last edn 1971
7. Mineral Railways Last edn 5th 1967
8. Light & N G Locos Last edn & 3rd 1954

Collected Edition (The Light Railway Handbook) last edn 6th 1971

A note typed up on the Kidners' manual typewriter listing the 'Light Railway Handbooks'.

Section Three

'B' Series

This series focuses on the Welsh and Isle of Man narrow gauge railways. Proposed titles in this series covering English, Scottish and Irish narrow gauge railways and a narrow gauge railway manual have not materialized. (NB: 'B1' and 'B2' are not official Oakwood references, but these titles do really belong in this series hence their inclusion here.)

James I.C. Boyd (1921-2009) was the author of all of the 'B' series titles. He was involved with the Talyllyn Railway during the early years of the preservation society, working there at weekends as a volunteer. James Boyd's reminsicences were published by Oakwood in two volumes as *Saga by Rail* (RS16 & RS17 - *see page 78*).

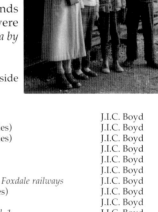

Above right: James Boyd, with his family, pose alongside *Douglas* on the Talyllyn Railway.

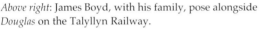

B1	*Narrow Gauge Rails to Porthmadoc*	J.I.C. Boyd
B1A	*Festiniog Railway Vol. 1 1800-1889 (variations in titles)*	J.I.C. Boyd
B1B	*Festiniog Railway Vol. 2 1890-1959 (variations in titles)*	J.I.C. Boyd
B2	*Isle of Man Railway*	J.I.C. Boyd
B2A	*Isle of Man Railway Vol. 1 pre-1873-1904*	J.I.C. Boyd
B2B	*Isle of Man Railway Vol. 2 1905-1994*	J.I.C. Boyd
B2C	*Isle of Man Railway Vol. 3 including Manx Northern, Foxdale railways*	J.I.C. Boyd
B3A	*Narrow Gauge Rails in Mid-Wales (variations in titles)*	J.I.C. Boyd
B4	*Narrow Gauge Railways in South Caernarvonshire*	J.I.C. Boyd
B4A	*Narrow Gauge Railways in South Caernarvonshire Vol. 1*	J.I.C. Boyd
B4B	*Narrow Gauge Railways in South Caernarvonshire Vol. 2*	J.I.C. Boyd
B5A	*Narrow Gauge Railways in North Caernarvonshire Vol. 1*	J.I.C. Boyd
B5B	*Narrow Gauge Railways in North Caernarvonshire Vol. 2*	J.I.C. Boyd
B5C	*Narrow Gauge Railways in North Caernarvonshire Vol. 3*	J.I.C. Boyd

B1 - 1949	B1A - 1956	B1A - 1960 - 2nd	B1A - 1965

B1A - 1975

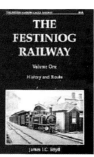

B1A - 2002

B1B - 1959

B1B - 1962

B1B - 1975

B1B - 2002

B2 - 1962

B2 - 1967 - 2nd

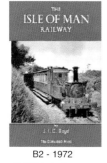

B2 - 1972

B2 - 1973

B2 - 1977

B2A - 1993

B2B - 1994

B2C - 1996

B3A - 1952

B3A - 1965

B3A - 1970 - 2nd

B3A - 1986

B4 - 1972

B4A - 1988

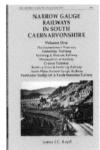

B4A - 2000

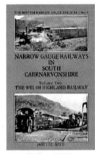

B4B - 1969

B4B - 1994

B5A - 1981

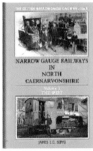

B5A - 1990

B5B - 1985

B5B - 2001

B5C - 1986

B5C - 2001

Section Four

'C' Series –
Canal Histories

This series gives an insight into various canals and waterways, with some tramroad and railway interest (NB: 'C1D' is not an official Oakwood reference but completes the C1A-C1C series).

C1A	*English Canals Part I: A Concise History*	D.D. Gladwin & J.M. White
C1B	*English Canals Part II: Engineers and Engineering*	D.D. Gladwin & J.M. White
C1C	*English Canals Part III: Boats and Boatmen*	D.D. Gladwin & J.M. White
C1D	*English Canals* (Parts I, II, III in one volume)	D.D. Gladwin & J.M. White
C2	*Wilts & Berks Canal*	L.J. Dalby
C3	*Canals of the Welsh Valleys and their Tramroads*	D.D. & J.M. Gladwin
C4	*Rowing Holiday by Canal in 1873 (Oxford - Oxford etc.)*	A. Farrant (ed. Dr E. Course)
C5	*Passenger Boats on Inland Waterways*	D.D. Gladwin
C6	*Horncastle & Tattershall Canal*	J.N. Clarke
C7	*Caldon Canal & Tramroads incl. Uttoxeter-Leek Canals etc.*	P. Lead
C8	*Hereford & Gloucester Canal* (1979 1st. ed not Oakwood)	D. Bick
C9	*Shakespeare's Avon: The History of a Navigation*	J. Davies
C10	*Navigation on the Yorkshire Derwent*	P. Jones

C1A - 1967

C1A - 197?

C1B - 1968

C1B - 197?

C1C - 1969

C1C - 197?

C1D - 1970

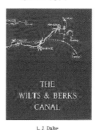

C2 - 1971 - 90p

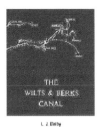

C2 - 1974 (rp1971)

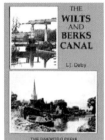

C2 - 1986

C2 - 1989 (rp1986)

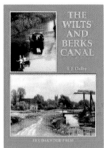

C2 - 2000

C3 - 1975

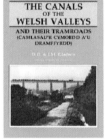

C3 - 1991

C4 - 1977

C5 - 1980

C6 - 1990

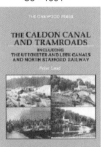

C7 - 1990

C8 - 1994 - 2nd

C8 - 2003 - 3rd

C9 - 1996

C10 - 2000

Section Five

'LP' Series –
Locomotion Papers

With the decision not to revive the *Locomotion* magazine and print occasional 'Locomotion Papers' instead, 1947 saw the printing of the first in the series, LP1 *The Alford & Sutton Tramway*, which had just 20 pages. LP1 was also subtitled '*Locomotion* Vol. X1 No. 35 July 1947', following on the sequence from the last *Locomotion* magazine No. 34, LP2 and LP3 carried on this practice with *Locomotion* Vol. X1 Nos. 36 and 37, but after this the subtitling stopped.

The Locomotion Papers were started as a series of original research articles into the history of transport in the United Kingdom, by rail, road, water and air, which were really too long or too specialized for magazines and too short to appear as books. Most of the early titles were really small booklets, but over the years they have evolved and a few titles in the series now run to over 200 pages.

Early plans included two titles *Early Roads in Northern Scotland* by H.A. Vallance and *Building the Woodhead Tunnel* by Jack Simmons. Unfortunately these did not appear and also no aviation titles have yet been published in the LP series although the 'X' series does include an aviation title.

This excellent series covers a fascinating range of transport titles with the emphasis on railways, but also covering road and tram titles. It has now reached LP235, which is also the first LP title to run to over 300 pages, a long way from the original 20 page booklet.

LP1	*Alford & Sutton Tramway* (1984 ed. not Oakwood)	G. Dow
LP2	*Railways to Cambridge: Actual and Proposed* (1976 ed. not Oakwood)	R.B. Fellows
LP3	*Steam Lorry 1896-1939* ('1896-1939' only on 1948 edition)	R.W. Kidner
LP4	*Channel Tunnel and Ferry*	J.L. Harrington
LP5	*London Motor Bus 1896-1949* (1953/62/8/75/9)	R.W. Kidner
LP6	*Southern Railway 1923-1947: A Chronicle and Record*	R.A. Savill
LP7	*London Tramcar 1861-1951* ('1861-1952' title from 1956 edition)	R.W. Kidner
LP8	*Traction Engine 1842-1936* ('1842-1936' only on 1966 edition)	F.H. Gillford
LP9	*History of the Steam Tram* (based on 1937 Paper) (2000 ed. not Oakwood)	H.A. Whitcombe
LP10	*Cromford & High Peak Railway*	A. Rimmer
LP11	*Development of the Trolley Bus* (Trolley Bus 1882-1966, 1882-1972)	H. Brearley
LP12	*Development of the Railcar* (updated version of A21)	R.W. Kidner
LP13	*Tramways in West Yorkshire*	H. Brearley
LP14	*Battery Traction on Tramways and Railways*	T. Illingworth
LP15	*North Eastern Railway Electrics* (NB:. LP165, LP167)	K. Hoole
LP16	*Axholme Joint Railway* (NB: OL92)	G. Oates
LP17	*Historical Notes on the Railways of South East Monmouthshire*	A.J. Pritchard
LP18	*Glyn Valley Tramway* (1991 ed. revised R.W. Kidner)	D.L. Davies
LP19	*Lee Moor Tramway*	R.M.S. Hall
LP20	*Dublin & Blessington Tramway*	H. Fayle & A.T. Newham
LP21	*Cleobury Mortimer & Ditton Priors Light Railway*	M.R.C. Price
LP22	*Mid-Suffolk Light Railway*	N.A. Comfort
LP23	*Garstang & Knott End Railway*	R.W. Rush & M.R.C. Price
LP24	*Schull & Skibbereen Tramway* (NB: OL108)	A.T. Newham
LP25	*Weston, Clevedon & Portishead Light Railway*	C.G. Maggs
LP26	*Trafford Park Tramways*	E. Gray

LP27	Showman's Engines	W. Pickles
LP28	Saundersfoot Railway	M.R.C. Price
LP29	Dublin & Lucan Tramway	A.T. Newham
LP30	Ashover Light Railway	K.P. Plant
LP31	Bioscope Shows and their Engines	A. Fay
LP32	Lambourn Valley Railway	M.R.C. Price
LP33	Listowel & Ballybunion Railway (1989 ed. updated by M. Foster)	A.T. Newham
LP34	Dartford Loop Line 1866-1966 ('1866-1966' not on 1982 edition)	R.W. Kidner
LP35	Romney, Hythe & Dymchurch Railway	R.W. Kidner
LP36	North Sunderland Railway	A. Wright
LP37	Derwent Valley (Light*) Railway (1967*)1978 ed. revised by D.S.M. Barrie	S.J. Reading
LP38	Peak Forest Tramway (1989, 1995 ed. including Peak Forest Canal)	D. Ripley
LP39	Cork & Muskerry Light Railway (1992 ed. revised by S.C. Jenkins)	A.T. Newham
LP40	Davington Light Railway	M.M. Taylor
LP41	Portstewart Tramway	J.R.L. Currie
LP42	London Country Bus	J.S. Wagstaff
LP43	Gloucester & Cheltenham Railway (Tramroad) and the Leckhampton Quarry Lines	D.E. Bick
LP44	Ravenglass & Eskdale Railway	P. E.B. Butler & J.D. Lyne
LP45	Campbeltown & Machrihanish Light Railway	A.D. Farr
LP46	Easingwold Railway (1991 ed. revised by R.N. Redman)	K.E. Hartley
LP47	East Kent Railway	A.R. Catt
LP48	Great Western London Suburban Services (1948 ed. not Oakwood)	T.B. Peacock
LP49	Cork, Blackrock & Passage Railway (1993 ed. revised by S.C. Jenkins)	A.T. Newham
LP50	Swansea & Mumbles Railway (1942 ed. not Oakwood)	C.E. Lee
LP51	Lowgill Branch: A Lost Route to Scotland (NB: LP175 2nd edition)	R.G. Western
LP52	Bath Tramways	C.G. Maggs
LP53	British Steam Railcars	R.W. Rush
LP54	Life at Brighton Loco Works 1928-1936	A.C. Perryman
LP55	Nidd Valley Light Railway	D.J. Croft
LP56	Kent & East Sussex Railway	S.R. Garrett
LP57	London RT Bus: The Story of London's Longest-Lasting Bus	J.S. Wagstaff
LP58	Oxted Line (NB: OL123)	R.W. Kidner
LP59	Bournemouth Trams and Buses	C.G. Roberts
LP60	Pier Railways (1999 ed. and Tramways of the British Isles)	K. Turner
LP61	Cambridge Street Tramways	S.L. Swingle
LP62	London Independent Bus Operators 1922-1933	D.E. Brewster
LP63	Brookes Industrial Railways	S.A. Leleux
LP64	Brighton Baltics	A.C. Perryman
LP65	Swindon Tramways (1985 ed. and Electricity Undertaking)	L.J. Dalby
LP66	'Hants and Dorset' Buses	C.G. Roberts
LP67	My 70 Years with Traction Engines	W.G. Hooker
LP68	Railways of Purbeck	R.W. Kidner
LP69	Highbridge in its Heyday (1986 ed. Home of Somerset & Dorset Railway)	C.G. Maggs
LP70	Cement Railways of Kent	B.D. Stoyel & R.W. Kidner
LP71	Little Eaton Gangway 1793-1908 (1993 ed. and Derby Canal)	D. Ripley
LP72	Westerham Valley Railway	D. Gould
LP73	Kinver Light Railway	S.L. Swingle & K. Turner
LP74	Southern Railway Rolling Stock	R.W. Kidner
LP75	Wotton Tramway (Brill Branch)	K. Jones
LP76	Railways and Mineral Tramways of Rossendale	B. Roberts
LP77	Isle of Grain Railways	A. Gray
LP78	Weston-super-Mare Tramways	C.G. Maggs
LP79	Reading to Tonbridge Line	R.W. Kidner
LP80	Motor Buses in East Anglia 1901-1931	D.E. Brewster
LP81	Cardiff's Electric Tramways	D. Gould
LP82	Military Traction Engines and Lorries 1858-1918	R.W. Kidner
LP83	London Routemaster Bus	J.S. Wagstaff

LP84	*Travelling Shows and Roundabouts*	A. Sellman
LP85	*Motor Buses in London 1904-1908*	R.W. Kidner
LP86	(1985 ed. *Fairford Branch*) *Witney & East Gloucestershire Railway*	S.C. Jenkins
LP87	*Horsham-Guildford Direct Railway*	H.R. Hood
LP88	*Diesel Locomotives of the L.M.S.*	J.W.P. Rowledge
LP89	*Motor Buses in Wales 1898-1932*	D.E. Brewster
LP90	*Bradford Tramways*	D.J. Croft
LP91	*Lickey Incline* (1990 ed. revised by S.C. Jenkins)	H.C. Casserley
LP92	*Wantage Tramway* (1974 ed. not Oakwood)	R. Wilkinson
LP93	*Southern Railway Branch Lines in the Thirties*	R.W. Kidner
LP94	*Apprentice at McLaren's 1916-1920*	S.R. Fowler
LP95	*Lancaster & Morecambe Tramways*	S. Shuttleworth
LP96	*Elsenham & Thaxted Light Railway*	P. Paye
LP97	*Fireless Locomotives*	A.D.T. Civil & A. Baker
LP98	*British Battery Electric Buses*	D. Kaye
LP99	*Maunsell Moguls*	J.W.P. Rowledge
LP100	*Goole & Selby Railway*	C.T. Goode
LP101	*The London Single-Deck Bus of the Fifties*	J.S. Wagstaff
LP102	*Railways to Sevenoaks*	C. Devereux
LP103	*North Kent Line*	R.W. Kidner
LP104	*Buses on the Continent 1898-1976*	J.F.J. Kuipers
LP105	*Newport Trams*	C.G. Maggs
LP106	*Passenger Tramways of Pontypridd*	R. Large
LP107	*Sidmouth, Seaton and Lyme Regis Branches*	C.G. Maggs & P. Paye
LP108	*Tattenham Corner Branch*	N. Owen
LP109	*Carriage Stock of Minor Standard Gauge Railways*	R.W. Kidner
LP110	*Kings Cross in the Twenties*	W.R. Thrower
LP111	*Barnstaple & Ilfracombe Railway*	C.G. Maggs
LP112	*Leamington & Warwick Tramways*	S.L. Swingle & K. Turner
LP113	*Railways in the Sirhowy Valley*	W.W. Tasker
LP114	*North Warwickshire Railway*	C.T. Goode
LP115	*Bessbrook & Newry Tramway*	A.T. Newham
LP116	*Caldon Canal & Tramroads including Uttoxeter and Leek Canals and the North Staffordshire Railway*	P. Lead
LP117	*Newhaven and Seaford Branch*	R.W. Kidner
LP118	*Somerset & Dorset Engineman*	F.E. Stickley
LP119	*Hither Green Motive Power Depot*	N. Pallant
LP120	*Lymington Branch*	P. Paye
LP121	(*Industrial* 1988 ed.) *Railways of Port Sunlight and Bromborough Port*	M.D. Lister
LP122	*Railways to Exmouth* (NB: LP203)	C.G. Maggs
LP123	*Mellis & Eye Railway*	P. Paye
LP124	*Service Stock of the Southern Railway* (NB: X51)	R.W. Kidner
LP125	*Bricklayers Arms Branch and Loco Shed*	M. Jackman
LP126	*Taunton to Barnstaple Line - Devon & Somerset Railway*	C.G. Maggs
LP127	*North Midland Trains in the Thirties*	A.S. Denton
LP128	*Wensleydale Branch* (NB: OL86)	C.T. Goode
LP129	*Minor Standard Gauge Railways* (NB: A1A)	R.W. Kidner
LP130	*Bexleyheath Line*	E.A. Course
LP131	*Dursley Branch*	P. Smith
LP132	*Bridgwater Branch* (1990 ed. *Bridgwater Railway*)	J.D. Harrison
LP133	*Brighton to Portsmouth Line*	N. Pallant
LP134	*South Eastern & Chatham Railway in the 1914-18 War*	D. Gould
LP135	*Railways of East Yorkshire*	C.T. Goode
LP136	*Ely & St Ives Railway*	P. Paye
LP137	*Wye Valley Railway* (NB: LP209)	B.M. Handley
LP138	*Bath to Weymouth Line*	C.G. Maggs
LP139	*East Suffolk Railway*	J.M. Cooper

LP140	*Waterloo to Southampton Line*	R.W. Kidner
LP141	*Findhorn Railway*	I.K. Dawson
LP142	*Stoke to Market Drayton Line and associated canals and mineral branches*	C.R. Lester
LP143	*Brookwood Necropolis Railway*	J.M. Clarke
LP144	*Three Bridges to Tunbridge Wells*	D. Gould
LP145	*Banstead & Epsom Downs Railway*	J.R.W. Kirby
LP146	*Kettering-Huntingdon Line*	J. Rhodes
LP147	*Southern Suburban Steam (1860-1967)*	R.W. Kidner
LP148	*Great Northern Main Line*	W.R. Thrower
LP149	*Hertford Loop Line*	C.T. Goode
LP150	*Louth to Bardney Branch*	A.J. Ludlam & W.B. Herbert
LP151	*Gravesend West Branch*	N. Pallant
LP152	*Shenfield to Southend Line*	C. Phillips
LP153	*Southern Railway Branch Line Trains*	R.W. Kidner
LP154	*Spilsby to Firsby Railway*	A.J. Ludlam
LP155	*Corringham Light Railway*	I. Gotheridge
LP156	*Southern Railway Halts Survey and Gazetteer*	R.W. Kidner
LP157	*Branch Lines to Ramsey*	J. Rhodes
LP158	*Horncastle & Woodhall Junction Railway*	A.J. Ludlam
LP159	*Railways of Porthgain and Abereiddi*	R.C. Jermy
LP160	*Prestatyn and Dyserth Branch Line*	S.P. Goodall
LP161	*Brixham Branch*	C.R. Potts
LP162	*Louth, Mablethorpe and Willoughby Loop*	A.J. Ludlam
LP163	*Lincolnshire Potato Railways*	S.E. Squires
LP164	*Pullman Cars on the 'Southern' 1895-1972* (NB: No. LP210)	R.W. Kidner
LP165	*North Eastern Electrics,* *The History Tyneside Electric Passenger Services 1904-1967* (NB: LP15)	K. Hoole
LP166	*Colne Valley & Halstead Railway* (1951 ed. not Oakwood)	R. Whitehead & F.D. Simpson
LP167	*Electric Locomotives of the North Eastern Railway* (n.b. LP15)	K. Hoole
LP168	*Hatfield and St Albans Branch of the Great Northern Railway*	R.D. Taylor & B. Anderson
LP169	*RAF Cranwell Railway*	A.J. Ludlam
LP170	*USA 756th Railway Shops Battalion at Newport (Ebbw Jn)*	E.R. Mountford
LP171	*Leeds New Line - The Heaton Lodge and Wortley Railway*	R. Waring
LP172	*Bognor Branch Line* (printed with OL172 reference in error)	S. Jordan
LP173	*Moretonhampstead & South Devon Railway*	S.C. Jenkins & L.J. Pomeroy
LP174	*Rishworth Branch*	J.N. Fisher
LP175	*Ingleton Branch: A Lost Route to Scotland* (NB: LP51 1st edition)	R.G. Western
LP176	*Solway Junction Railway*	S. Edgar & J.M. Sinton
LP177	*Watford to St Albans Branch* (2008 ed. additions from G. Hughes)	S.C. Jenkins
LP178	*Melbourne Military Railway, The History of the Railway Training Centre at Melbourne and King's Newton 1939-1945*	Cooper, Leggott, & Sprenger
LP179	*Leek & Manifold Light Railway*	S.C. Jenkins
LP180	*Rothbury Branch*	S.C. Jenkins
LP181	*Melton Constable to Cromer Branch*	S.C. Jenkins
LP182	*Seaton Branch and Seaton Tramway*	C.G. Maggs
LP183	*Mangotsfield to Bath Branch* (2005 ed. *incl. Green Park Station*)	C.G. Maggs
LP184	*Helston Branch Railway* (NB: OL21)	S.C. Jenkins
LP185	*Taff Vale Lines to Penarth*	E.R. Mountford & N. Sprinks
LP186	*Catterick Camp Military Railway and the Richmond Branch*	A.J. Ludlam
LP187	*Llandudno & Colwyn Bay Electric Railway*	K. Turner
LP188	*Girvan & Portpatrick Junction Railway*	C.E.J. Fryer
LP189	*Tramways of Lytham St Annes*	Abell, Garnham & McLoughlin

LP190	*Lincolnshire Loop Line (GNR) and the River Witham*	A.J. Ludlam
LP191	*Lampeter, Aberayron & New Quay Light Railway*	M.R.C. Price
LP192	*Llantrisant Branches of the Taff Vale Railway*	C. Chapman
LP193	*Sidmouth and Budleigh Salterton Branches*	C.G. Maggs
LP194	*GWR and the General Strike (1926)*	C.R. Potts
LP195	*Lincoln to Grantham Line via Honington*	S.E. Squires
LP196	*Lauder Light Railway*	A.M. Hajducki & A. Simpson
LP197	*Harpenden to Hemel Hempstead Railway - The Nickey Line*	S.L. Woodward & G. Woodward
LP198	*Railways to New Holland and the Humber Ferries*	A.J. Ludlam
LP199	*Kingsbridge Branch - The Primrose Line (1977 ed. not Oakwood)*	K. Williams & D. Reynolds
LP200	*Nelson and Ynysybwl Branches of the Taff Vale Railway*	C. Chapman
LP201	*Eden Valley Railway*	R.G. Western
LP202	*Huddersfield and Kirkburton Branch*	J.N. Fisher
LP203	*Exeter & Exmouth Railway (NB: LP122)*	C.G. Maggs
LP204	*Gwendraeth Valleys Railway Kidwelly to Mynydd-y-Garreg*	M.R.C. Price
LP205	*Railways to Skegness including Kirkstead to Little Steeping*	A.J. Ludlam
LP206	*Minehead Branch and the West Somerset Railway*	C.G. Maggs
LP207	*Cirencester Branch*	N.S.M. Bray
LP208	*Vale of Glamorgan Railway*	C. Chapman
LP209	*Wye Valley Railway and the Coleford Branch (NB: LP137)*	B.M. Handley & R. Dingwall
LP210	*Pullman Trains in Britain (NB: replaced LP164 using part same)*	R.W. Kidner
LP211	*Glencorse Branch*	J. Hurst
LP212	*Winsford and Over Branch*	R.W. Miller
LP213	*Rails to Poole Harbour*	C. Stone
LP214	*Nailsworth and Stroud Branch*	C.G. Maggs
LP215	*Ely Valley Railway: Llantrisant to Penygraig*	C. Chapman
LP216	*Carrying Coals to Dunston, Coal and the Railway*	E. Manns
LP217	*Cairn Valley Light Railway, Moniaive to Dumfries*	I. Kirkpatrick
LP218	*Burntisland, Fife's Railway Port*	P. Marshall
LP219	*Yate to Thornbury Branch*	C.G. Maggs
LP220	*Ross Monmouth and Pontypool Road Line*	S.C. Jenkins
LP221	*Fawley Branch, The Story of the Totton Hythe & Fawley Light Railway*	J.R. Fairman
LP222	*Rails to Achill, A West of Ireland Branch Line*	J. Beaumont
LP223	*Cliff Railways of the British Isles*	K. Turner
LP224	*Wrington Vale Light Railway*	C.G. Maggs
LP225	*Railways of Upper Strathearn, Crieff-Balquhidder*	B. Byrom
LP226	*Wrexham & Ellesmere Railway*	S.C. Jenkins & J.M. Strange
LP227	*Horse Tramways of the British Isles*	R.W. Rush
LP228	*By Great Western to Crewe, Wellington to Nantwich and Crewe Line*	B. Yate
LP229	*Snape Branch*	P. Paye
LP230	*Hadleigh Branch*	P. Paye
LP231	*Culm Valley Light Railway, Tiverton Junction to Hemyock*	C.G. Maggs
LP232	*Coniston Railway*	R. Western
LP233	*Framlingham Branch*	P. Paye
LP234A	*Northern Northumberland's Minor Railways Volume One; Brickworks, Forestry, Contractors, Military Target railways and other various lines*	R. Jermy
LP234B	*Northern Northumberland's Minor Railways Volume Two, Colliery & Associated Lines*	R. Jermy
LP234C	*Northern Northumberland's Minor Railways Volume Three, Sandstone, Whinstone & Gravel Lines*	R. Jermy
LP235	*Bishop's Stortford, Dunmow & Braintree Branch (1981 ed. not Oakwood)*	P. Paye

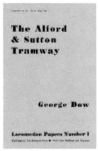

LP1 - 1947

LP1 - c.1963

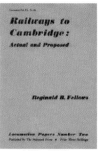

LP2 - 1948

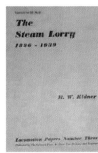

LP3 - 1948

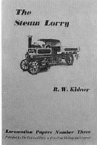

LP3 - 1956 - 2nd

LP3 - 1963

LP3 - c.1967

LP3 - c.1971

LP3 - c.1976

LP4 - 1949

LP5 - 1950

LP5 - 1953 - 2nd

LP5 - 1962 - 3rd

LP5 - 1968 - 4th

LP5 - 1975

LP5 - 1979

LP6 - 1950

LP7 - 1951

LP7 - 1955

LP7 - 1960

LP7 - c.1966 - 7s. 6d.

LP7 - 1970 - 10s./50p

LP7 - 1974

LP7 - 1976

LP7 - 1992

LP8 - 1952

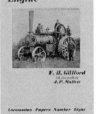

LP8 - 1966 - 5s.

LP8 - 1968 - 6s.

LP8 - c.1970

LP8 - c.1972

LP9 - 1954

LP9 - 1961 - 6s.

LP9 - 1970 - 8s./40p

LP10 - 1956 - 5s. 6d.

LP10 - 1960 - 5s. 6d.

LP10 - 1962 - 6s.

LP10 - 1967 - 7s. 6d.

LP10 - 1970 - 60p/12s.

LP10 - 1974 - 75p

LP10 - 1976 - 90p

LP10 - 1978 - £1.20

LP10 - 1980 - £1.50

LP10 - 1985

LP10 - 1988

LP10 - 1995

LP10 - 1998

LP11 - 1957

LP11 - 1966

LP11 - 1972

LP12 - 1958

LP13 - 1960

LP14 - 1961

LP15 - 1961

LP16 - 1961

LP17 - 1962

LP18 - 1962 - 12s. 6d.

LP18 - 1966 - 13s. 6d.

LP18 - c.1969 - 15s.

LP18 - 1974 - £1.80

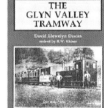

LP18 - 1991

LP19 - 1963

LP19 - 1979

LP19 - 1987

LP20 - 1963 - 8s. 6d.

LP20 - 1980

LP21 - 1963

LP21 - 1978

LP21 - 1995

LP22 - 1963 - 8s. 6d.

LP22 - 1972 - 60p

LP22 - 1977

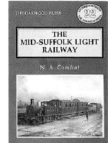

LP22 - 1986

LP22 - 1997

LP23 - 1964

LP23 - 1985

LP24 - 1964

LP25 - 1964* - 10s. 6d.
* Also 1970 overprinted
   12s. 6d./65p

LP25 - 1976 - £1.05

LP25 - 1979

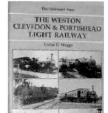

LP25 - 1990

LP26 - 1964

LP27 - 1964

LP27 - c.1970s

LP28 - 1964

LP28 - c.1971 - 30p

LP28 - 1975

LP28 - 1978

LP28 - 1989

LP29 - 1964

LP30 - 1965

LP30 - 1987

LP31 - 1966

LP32 - 1964

LP32 - 1976

LP33 - 1967 - 9s. 6d.

LP33 - c.1972 - 60p

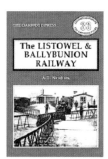

LP33 - 1989

LP34 - 1966

LP34 - 1976

LP34 - 1982

LP35 - 1967

LP35 - 1978

LP36 - 1967

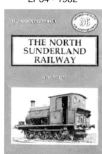

LP36 - 1988

LP37 - 1967

LP37 - 1976

LP37 - 1978

LP38 - 1968 - 7s. 6d.

LP38 - 1972 - 60p

LP38 - 1977 - 75p

LP38 - 1981 - £1.50

LP38 - 1989

LP38 - 1995

LP39 - 1968

LP39 - 1992

LP40 - 1968

LP40 - 1986

LP41 - 1968

LP41 - c.1970s

LP42 - 1968 - 15s.

LP42 - 1975 - £1.20

LP43 - 1968

LP43 - 1987

LP44 - 1969

LP45 - 1969

LP45 - 1987

LP46 - 1970

LP46 - 1991

LP47 - 1970 - 15s./75p

LP47 - c.1972 - £1.20

LP47 - 1975 - £1.70

LP48 - 1970

LP48 - 1978

LP49 - 1970

LP49 - 1993

LP50 - 1954

LP50 - 1970

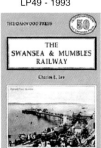

LP50 - c.1976

LP50 - 1988

LP51 - 1971

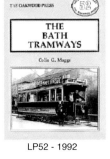

LP52 - 1971

LP52 - 1992

LP53 - 1971

LP53 - c.1979

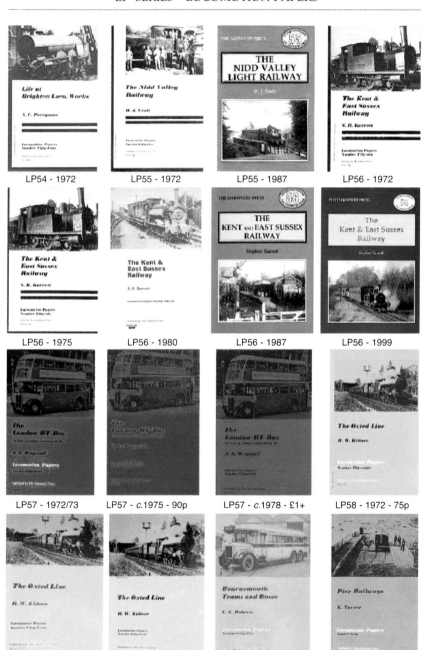

LP54 - 1972	LP55 - 1972	LP55 - 1987	LP56 - 1972
LP56 - 1975	LP56 - 1980	LP56 - 1987	LP56 - 1999
LP57 - 1972/73	LP57 - *c.*1975 - 90p	LP57 - *c.*1978 - £1+	LP58 - 1972 - 75p
LP58 - 1975	LP58 - 1982	LP59 - 1972	LP60 - 1972

LP60 - 1999

LP61 - 1972

LP62 - 1972

LP62 - 1975

LP63 - 1972

LP64 - 1973

LP64 - 1976

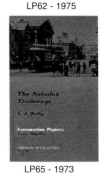

LP65 - 1973

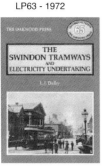

LP65 - 1985

LP66 - 1973

LP67 - 1973

LP68 - 1973

LP68 - 1979

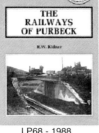

LP68 - 1988

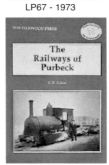

LP68 - 2000

LP69 - 1973

LP69 - *c.*1975

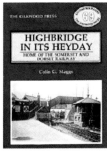

LP69 - 1986

LP70 - 1973

LP70 - *c.*1979

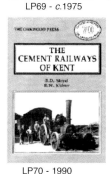

LP70 - 1990

LP71 - 1973

LP71 - 1993

LP72 - 1974

LP72 - 1976

LP72 - 1981

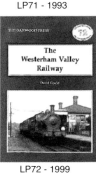

LP72 - 1999

LP73 - 1974

LP73 - 1987

LP74 - 1974

LP74 - 1976

LP75 - 1974

LP75 - 1979

LP76 - 1974

LP77 - 1974

LP77 - 1976

LP78 - 1974

LP79 - 1974

LP79 - c.1979

LP80 - 1974

LP81 - 1974

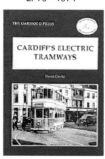

LP81 - 1996

LP82 - 1975

LP83 - 1975 - 90p

LP83 - 1979 - £1.05

LP84 - 1975

LP85 - 1975

LP86 - 1975

LP86 - 1985

LP87 - 1975

LP88 - 1975

LP89 - 1976

LP90 - 1976

LP91 - 1976

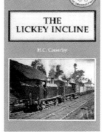

LP91 - 1990

LP92 - 1976

LP92 - 1995

LP93 - 1976

LP94 - 1976

LP95 - 1976

The Elsenham
& Thaxted
Light Railway

LP96 - 1976

Fireless
Locomotives

LP97 - 1976

British Battery
Electric Buses

LP98 - 1976

The Maunsell
Moguls

LP99 - 1976

LP100 - 1976

LP101 - 1976

LP102 - 1977

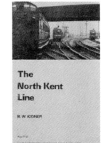

LP103 - 1977

LP104 - 1977

LP105 - 1977

LP106 - 1977

LP107 - 1977 - £1.50

LP107 - 1979 - £1.80

LP107 - c.1980s - £2.40

LP108 - 1978

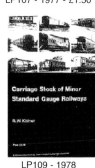

LP109 - 1978

LP110 - 1978

LP111 - 1978

LP111 - 1988

LP111 - 1994

LP112 - 1978

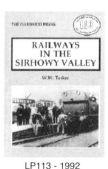

LP113 - 1978

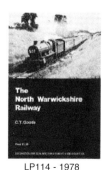

LP113 - 1992

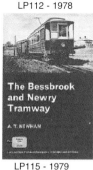

LP114 - 1978

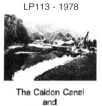

LP115 - 1979

LP116 - 1979

LP117 - 1979

LP118 - 1979

LP119 - 1979

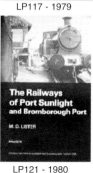

LP120 - 1979

LP121 - 1980

LP121 - 1988

LP122 - 1980

LP123 - 1980

LP124 - 1980

LP125 - 1980

LP126 - 1980

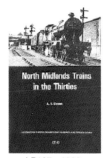

LP127 - 1980

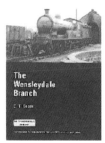

LP128 - 1980

LP129 - 1981

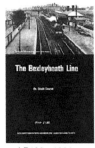

LP130 - 1981

LP131 - 1981

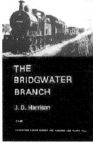

LP132 - 1981

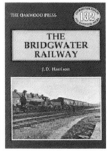

LP132 - 1990

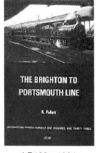

LP133 - 1981

LP134 - 1981

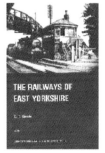

LP135 - 1981

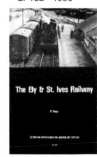

LP136 - 1982

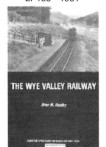

LP137 - 1982

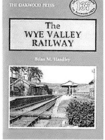

LP137 - 1988

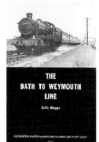

LP138 - 1982

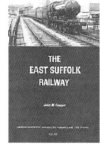

LP139 - 1982

LP140 - 1983

THE FINDHORN RAILWAY

LP141 - 1983

LP142 - 1983

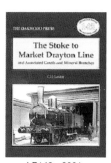

LP142 - 2001

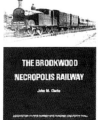

LP143 - 1983

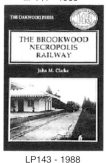

LP143 - 1988

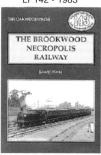

LP143 - 1995

LP143 - 2006

LP144 - 1983

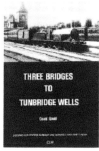

LP145 - 1983

LP146 - 1984

LP147 - 1984

LP148 - 1984

LP149 - 1984

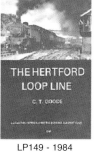

LP150 - 1984

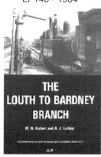

LP150 - 1987

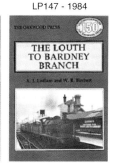

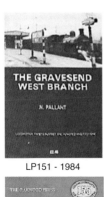
LP151 - 1984

LP152 - 1984

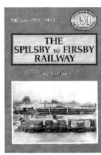
LP153 - 1984

LP154 - 1985

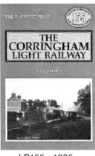
LP155 - 1985

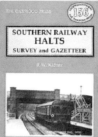
LP156 - 1985

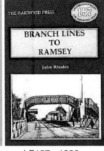
LP157 - 1986

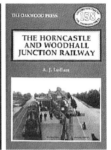
LP158 - 1986

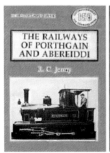
LP159 - 1986

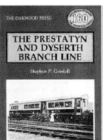
LP160 - 1986

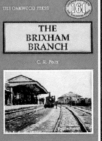
LP161 - 1986

LP161 - 2000

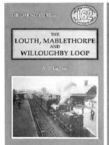
LP162 - 1987

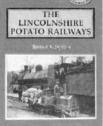
LP163 - 1987

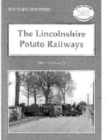
LP163 - 2005

LP164 - 1987

LP165 - 1987   LP166 - 1988   LP167 - 1988   LP168 - 1988

LP169 - 1988   LP170 - 1989   LP171 - 1989   LP172 - 1989

LP173 - 1989   LP174 - 1990   LP175 - 1990   LP176 - 1990

LP176 - 1993   LP177 - 1990   LP177 - 2008   LP178 - 1990

LP179 - 1991   LP180 - 1991   LP181 - 1991   LP182 - 1992

LP183 - 1992   LP183 - 2005   LP184 - 1992   LP184 - 2011

LP185 - 1993   LP186 - 1993   LP187 - 1993   LP187 - 2007

LP188 - 1994   LP189 - 1995   LP190 - 1995   LP191 - 1995

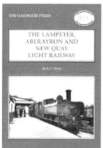

LP191 - 2011   LP192 - 1996   LP193 - 1996   LP194 - 1996

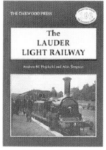
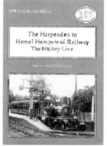

LP195 - 1996   LP196 - 1996   LP197 - 1996   LP197 - 2002

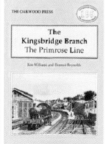
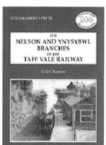
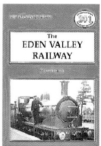

LP198 - 1996   LP199 - 1997   LP200 - 1997   LP201 - 1997

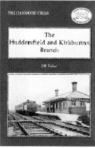
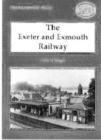
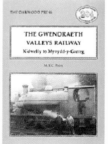

LP202 - 1997   LP203 - 1997   LP204 - 1997   LP205 - 1997

LP206 - 1998   LP206 - 2011   LP207 - 1998   LP208 - 1998

LP209 - 1998   LP209 - 2000   LP209 - 2007   LP210 - 1998

LP210 - 2005   LP211 - 1999   LP212 - 1999   LP213 - 1999

LP213 - 2007   LP214 - 2000   LP215 - 2000   LP216 - 2000

LP217 - 2000

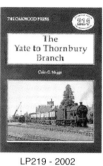

LP218 - 2001

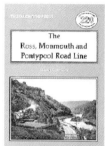

LP219 - 2002

LP220 - 2002

LP220 - 2009

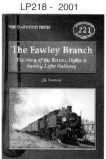

LP221 - 2002

LP222 - 2002

LP222 - 2005

LP223 - 2002

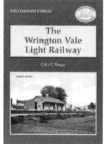

LP224 - 2004

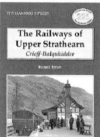

LP225 - 2004

LP226 - 2004

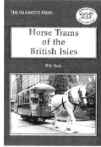

LP227 - 2004

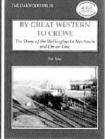

LP228 - 2005

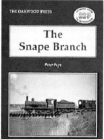

LP229 - 2005

LP230 - 2006

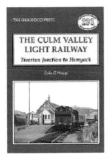

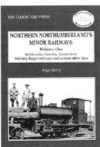

LP231 - 2006   LP232 - 2007   LP233 - 2008   LP234A - 2010

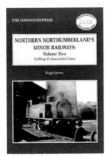
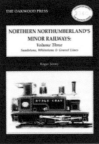

LP234B - 2011   LP234C - 2011   LP235 - 2010

Section Six

'MS' Series

The 'MS' series are all written by Mike Sharman. Editions marked with an asterisk were published by the author but distributed by Oakwood Press (NB: 'MS0' is not an official reference, but it is included here for completeness).

MS0	*Guide to Locomotive Building from Prototype to Small Scale Models*	M. Sharman
MS1	*Crampton Locomotive*	M. Sharman
MS2	*Flexichas - A Way to Build Fully Compensated Chassis*	
	(Also 1983/1986/1997 editions)	M. Sharman
MS2A	*Flexichas* (French Language Version)	M. Sharman
MS3	*Gear Fitting - for the Small Modeller with No Workshop*	M. Sharman
MS4	*Wheel Specifications for the Modeller*	
	(1978 1st ed. not Sharman or Oakwood)	M. Sharman

MS0 - 1986*

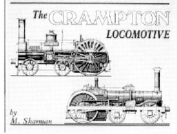

MS1 - 1983*

MS2 - 1982 - 1st

MS2 - 1988 - 4th

MS2 - 1999 - 4th rp

MS2A - 1996

MS3 - 1984

MS3 - 1988

MS4 - 1982 - 2nd*

MS4 - 1986 - 3rd*

MS4 - 1991 - 3rd rp

Section Seven

'OL' Series –
Oakwood Library of Railway History

An important and well presented series of histories that focus mainly on the smaller British railways, but latterly has also included some interesting biographies on railwaymen. The first title, *The North London Railway* (OL1), was published in September 1937 starting the OL series which now runs to over 150 titles, many of which have been reprinted several times.

There was a gap of several years between the publishing of OL2 and OL3 because both editors R. Michael Robbins and R.W. Kidner were in the army.

OL1-17 were published in both softback and hardback editions. Notice also that OL51-OL59 were published out of sequence as the start of a new series in a slightly different format, these were bound with boards and quarter cloth, but this idea was not carried on and the original OL sequence was then eventually completed. This explains why the publication dates do not follow the numerical order in this portion of the OL series. Look out also for OL172: this reference was printed in error on the front cover of LP172 *Bognor Branch Line*.

OL1	*North London Railway*	R.M. Robbins
OL2	*Taff Vale Railway*	D.S.M. Barrie
OL3	*Hull & Barnsley Railway*	G.D. Parkes
OL4	*Maryport & Carlisle Railway*	J. Simmons
OL5	*Cheshire Lines Railway* (1978 ed. with additions from C.T. Goode)	R.P. Griffiths
OL6	*Somerset & Dorset Railway*	D.S.M. Barrie & C.R. Clinker
OL7	*Metropolitan Railway*	C. Baker
OL8	*London Tilbury & Southend Railway*	H.D. Welch
OL9	*Rhymney Railway* (1999 ed. author R.W. Kidner)	D.S.M. Barrie
OL10	*Stratford-upon-Avon & Midland Junction Railway* (1977 ed. *Stratford & Midland Junction Railway*)	J.M. Dunn
OL11	*City & South London Railway*	T.S. Lascelles
OL12	*Metropolitan District Railway*	C.E. Lee
OL13	*Brecon & Merthyr Railway* (1991 ed. revised R.W. Kidner)	D.S.M. Barrie
OL14	*Wrexham, Mold & Connah's Quay Railway* (NB: OL83)	J.M. Dunn
OL15	*Belfast & County Down Railway* (1982 ed. not Oakwood)	E.M. Patterson
OL16	*Midland & South Western Junction Railway* (1990 ed. revised S.C. Jenkins)	T.B. Sands
OL17	*Wirral Railway*	C. Highet
OL18	*Mersey Railway*	G.W. Parkin
OL19	*Lancashire, Derbyshire & East Coast Railway*	J. Cupit & W. Taylor
OL20	*Plymouth, Devonport & South Western Junction Railway*	A.J. Cheesman
OL21	*Hayle, West Cornwall and Helston Railways* (NB: LP184, OL122)	G.H. Anthony
OL22	*West London Railway and the W.L.E.R.*	H.V. Borley & R.W. Kidner
OL23	*Plymouth & Dartmoor Railway*	H.G. Kendall
OL24	*North Pembroke & Fishguard Railway*	J.P. Morris
OL25	*Chester & Holyhead Railway* (NB: X5)	J.M. Dunn
OL26	*Bristol & Gloucester Railway and the Avon & Gloucestershire Railway*	C.G. Maggs
OL27	*Canterbury & Whitstable Railway*	I. Maxted
OL28	*Didcot, Newbury & Southampton Railway*	T.B. Sands
OL29	*Tavistock, Launceston & Princetown Railways* (1997 *Launceston Branch*)	G.H. Anthony
OL30	*Preston & Longridge Railway*	N. Parker
OL31	*Brampton Railway*	J.N. Charters

OL32	*Mawddwy, Van and Kerry Railways* (2004 ed. author with Kidner, Poole)	L. Cozens
OL33	*South Yorkshire Joint Railway* (2002 ed. *and the Coalfield*)	B.J. Elliott
OL34	*Manchester South Junction & Altrincham Railway*	F. Dixon
OL35	*Furness Railway 1843-1923*	R.W. Rush
OL35A	*Furness Railway Locomotives and Rolling Stock*	R.W. Rush
OL36	*Bolton, Blackburn, Clitheroe & West Yorkshire Railway*	W.D. Tattershall
OL37	*Bristol Port Railway and Pier*	C.G. Maggs
OL38	*Railways of Mid-Sussex*	A. Gray
OL39	*Whitland & Cardigan Railway*	M.R.C. Price
OL40	*Oxford Worcester & Wolverhampton Railway*	S. Jenkins & H. Quayle
OL41	*Malmesbury Railway*	D.M. Fenton
OL42	*Railways, Canals & Mines of Looe & Liskeard 1841-1977*	L. Popplewell
OL43	*London to Brighton Line 1841-1977*	A. Gray
OL44	*Hatfield, Luton & Dunstable Railway and onto Leighton Buzzard*	G. & S. Woodward
OL45	*Felixstowe Railway*	H.I. Quayle
OL46	*Great Western & Great Central Joint Railway*	S.C. Jenkins
OL47	*Cheadle Railway*	A.C. Baker
OL48	*Tanat Valley Light Railway* (1968 ed. not Oakwood)	W.J. Wren
OL49	*Hayling Railway*	P. Paye
OL50	*Manchester & Milford Railway*	J.S. Holden
OL51	*Lynton & Barnstaple Railway 1895-1935*	L.T. Catchpole
OL51A	*Locomotive Work on the Lynton & Barnstaple Railway*	F.E. Box
OL52	*London, Chatham & Dover Railway*	R.W. Kidner
OL53	*South Eastern Railway and S.E.C.R* *(South Eastern & Chatham Railway 1963, 1978)*	R.W. Kidner
OL54	*Isle of Wight Railways* (NB: OL109, OL115, OL125 and OL140)	M. Robbins
OL55	*Cambrian Railways*	R.W. Kidner
OL56	*Southern Railway*	R.W. Kidner
OL57	*Barry Railway*	D.S.M. Barrie
OL58	*Jersey Railway (J.R.& T.)*	N.R.P. Bonsor
OL58A	*Jersey Eastern Railway & German Occupation Lines in Jersey* (NB: OL143)	N.R.P. Bonsor
OL58B	*Guernsey Railway, German Occupation Lines and Alderney Railway*	N.R.P. Bonsor
OL59	*Glasgow & South Western Railway*	C. Highet
OL60	*Dundalk, Newry & Greenore Railway* (1st ed. published out of sequence)	D.S.M. Barrie
OL61	*Stafford & Uttoxeter Railway*	P. Jones
OL62	*South Devon Railway*	R.H. Gregory
OL63	*West Lancashire Railway*	J.E. Cotterall
OL64	*St Helens Railway, Its Rivals and Successors*	J.M. Tolson
OL65	*East Lancashire Railway*	R.W. Rush
OL66	*Caterham Railway, The story of a feud and its aftermath* (1st ed. as OL60)	J. Spence
OL67	*Great Northern Railway of Ireland* (NB: X1)	E.M. Patterson
OL68	*Pembroke & Tenby Railway*	M.R.C. Price
OL69	*Cardiff Railway*	E.R. Mountford
OL70	*Lynn & Hunstanton Railway & the West Norfolk Branch*	S.C. Jenkins
OL71	*Elan Valley Railway,* *The railway of the Birmingham Corporation Waterworks*	C.W. Judge
OL72	*Wirksworth Branch*	H. Sprenger
OL73	*Wells-Next-the-Sea Branch via Wymondham and Dereham*	S.C. Jenkins
OL74	*Cromer Branch*	S.C. Jenkins
OL75	*Newton Abbot to Kingswear Railway (1844-1988)*	C.R. Potts
OL76	*Callander & Oban Railway*	C.E.J. Fryer
OL77	*Balerno Branch and the Caley in Edinburgh*	D. Shaw
OL78	*Northampton & Banbury Junction Railway*	S.C. Jenkins
OL79	*Mid-Wales Railway*	R.W. Kidner
OL80	*Alston Branch*	S.C. Jenkins
OL81	*Portpatrick & Wigtownshire Railways*	C.E.J. Fryer
OL82	*East Lincolnshire Railway*	A.J. Ludlam
OL83	*Wrexham, Mold & Connah's Quay Railway,* *including the Buckley Railway* (NB: OL14)	J.I.C.Boyd

OL84	*Llanelly & Mynydd Mawr Railway*	M.R.C. Price
OL85	*North Berwick and Gullane Branch Lines*	A.M. Hajducki
OL86	*Wensleydale Branch, A New History* (NB: LP128)	S.C. Jenkins
OL87	*Lynn & Dereham Railway*	S.C. Jenkins
OL88	*Windsor to Slough: A Royal Branch Line*	C.R. Potts
OL89	*Bideford, Westward Ho! & Appledore Railway*	S.C. Jenkins
OL90	*Haddington, Macmerry and Gifford Branch Lines*	A.M. Hajducki
OL91	*Harton Electric Railway*	W.J. Hatcher
OL92	*Axholme Joint Railway, Goole & Marshland,*	
	Isle of Axholme Light Railways (NB: LP16)	C.W. Judge
OL93	*Whipsnade & Umfolozi Railway and the Great Whipsnade Railway*	C.S. Thomas
OL94	*Dundee & Newtyle Railway including Alyth & Blairgowrie Branches*	N. Ferguson
OL95	*Aberdare Railway*	E. Mountford &
		R.W. Kidner
OL96	*Leighton Buzzard Light Railway* (NB: X21)	S.A. Leleux
OL97	*Railways of Dundee*	P. Marshall
OL98	*J.G. Robinson: A Lifetime's Work*	D. Jackson
OL99	*Rails to Kyle of Lochalsh, the story of the Dingwall & Skye Railway*	D. McConnell
OL100	*Wemyss Private Railway*	A.W. Brotchie
OL101	*Scottish Central Railway: Perth to Stirling*	P. Marshall
OL102	*Richard Maunsell: An Engineering Biography*	J. Chacksfield
OL103	*Bridport Railway* (contains part of 1976 ed. not pub. by Oakwood)	B.L. Jackson &
		M.J. Tattershall
OL104	*Railways of Stourbridge*	C. Butcher
OL105	*Wenlock Branch, Wellington to Craven Arms*	K.B. Jones
OL106A	*Isle of Portland Railways Vol. 1 Admiralty and Quarry Railways*	B.L. Jackson
OL106B	*Isle of Portland Railways*	
	Vol. 2 Weymouth, Portland, Easton & Church Hope Railways	B.L. Jackson
OL106C	*Isle of Portland Rlys.Vol.3 Railway and Associated Bus Services*	B.L. Jackson
OL107	*Railways of Newark-on-Trent*	M. Vanns
OL108	*Schull & Skibbereen Railway* (NB: LP24)	J.I.C. Boyd
OL109	*Isle of Wight Railway* (n.b. OL54)	R.J. Maycock &
		R. Silsbury
OL110	*Sir Henry Fowler, A Versatile Life*	J. Chacksfield
OL111	*Waterford & Limerick Railway*	C.E.J. Fryer
OL112	*Arbroath & Forfar Railway Dundee Direct Line and the Kirriemuir Branch*	N. Ferguson
OL113	*Cockermouth, Keswick & Penrith Railway*	R. Western
OL114	*Sir William Stanier, A New Biography*	J. Chacksfield
OL115	*Isle of Wight Central Railway* (NB: OL54)	R.J. Maycock &
		R. Silsbury
OL116A	*Burry Port & Gwendreath Valley Railway and its antecedents Canals*	
	Vol. 1 Canals	R. Bowen
OL116B	*Burry Port & Gwendreath Valley Railway and its antecedent Canals*	
	Vol. 2 The Railway and Dock	R.W. Miller
OL117	*Waterloo & City Railway*	J.C. Gillham
OL118	*Sir Nigel Gresley the Engineer and His Family*	G. Hughes
OL119	*Caley to the Coast, or Rothesay to Weymss Bay*	A.J.C. Clark
OL120	*South Shields, Marsden & Whitburn Colliery Railway*	W.J. Hatcher
OL121	*C.B. Collett, A Competent Successor*	J. Chacksfield
OL122	*West Cornwall Railway: Truro to Penzance* (NB: OL21)	S.C. Jenkins &
		R.C. Langley
OL123	*Croydon, Oxted & East Grinstead Railway* (NB: LP58)	D. Gould
OL124	*Coey/Cowie Brothers, All Railwaymen*	J. Chacksfield
OL125	*Freshwater, Yarmouth & Newport Railway* (NB: OL54)	R.J. Maycock &
		R. Silsbury
OL126A	*Farranfore to Valentia Harbour Vol. 1 Plans, Construction, Operation*	P. O'Sullivan
OL126B	*Farranfore to Valentia Harbour Vol. 2 Services, Locomotives, Personalities*	P. O'Sullivan
OL127A	*East Kent Railway Vol. 1 History Of Independent Railway* (NB: LP247)	M. Lawson Finch
		& S.R. Garrett
OL127B	*East Kent Railway Vol. 2 Nationalisation, Route, Rolling Stock, Operation*	M. Lawson Finch

OL1 - 1937

OL1 - 1938

OL1 - 1946

OL1 - 1953

OL1 - 1959 - 5th

OL1 - 1967 - 7s. 6d.

OL1 - 1974 - 7th - 75p

OL1 - c.1980

OL1 - 1983 - 9th

OL2 - 1939

OL2 - 1950

OL2 - 1962

OL2 - 1969

OL2 - c.1970s

OL2 - 1977 - £1.50

OL2 - 1982 - £2.40

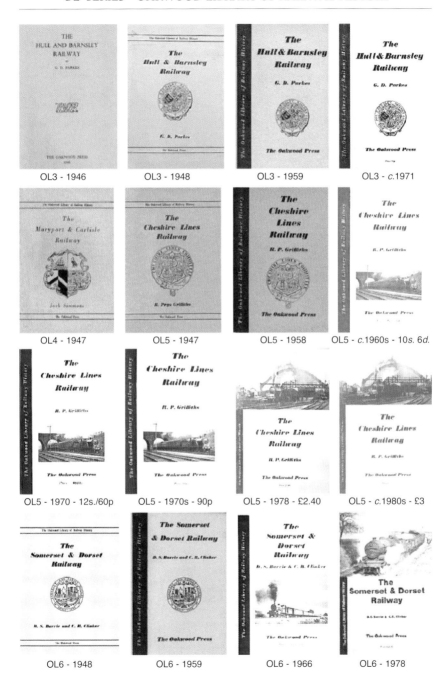

OL3 - 1946   OL3 - 1948   OL3 - 1959   OL3 - c.1971

OL4 - 1947   OL5 - 1947   OL5 - 1958   OL5 - c.1960s - 10s. 6d.

OL5 - 1970 - 12s./60p   OL5 - 1970s - 90p   OL5 - 1978 - £2.40   OL5 - c.1980s - £3

OL6 - 1948   OL6 - 1959   OL6 - 1966   OL6 - 1978

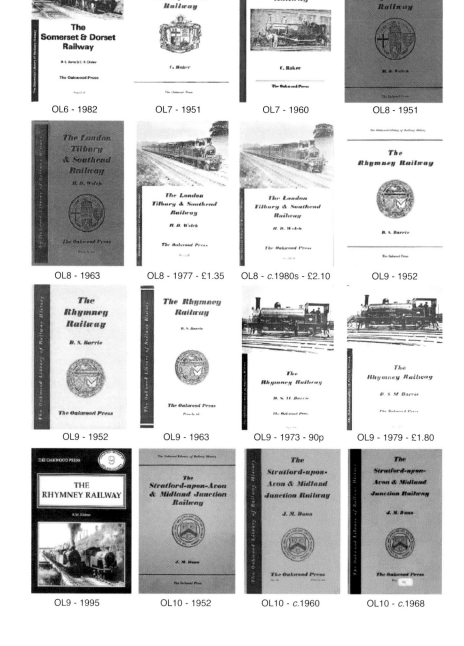

OL6 - 1982   OL7 - 1951   OL7 - 1960   OL8 - 1951

OL8 - 1963   OL8 - 1977 - £1.35   OL8 - *c.*1980s - £2.10   OL9 - 1952

OL9 - 1952   OL9 - 1963   OL9 - 1973 - 90p   OL9 - 1979 - £1.80

OL9 - 1995   OL10 - 1952   OL10 - *c.*1960   OL10 - *c.*1968

OL10 - 1977   OL11 - 1955   OL11 - 1987   OL12 - 1956

OL12 - 1988   OL13 - 1957   OL13 - 1965   OL13 - 1973

OL13 - 1975 - £1.35   OL13 - 1980 - £2+   OL13 - 1991   OL14 - 1957

OL15 - 1958   OL16 - 1959 - 10s. 6d.   OL16 - c.1960s - 14s. 6d.   OL16 - c.1970s - £1.20

OL16 - 1975 - £1.80   OL16 - 1979 - £2+   OL16 - 1990   OL17 - 1961

OL18 - 1965   OL19 - 1966 - 12s. 6d.   OL19 - 1984 - £2.70   OL19 - 1988

OL20 - 1967 - 10s. 6d.   OL20 - 1977 - £1.35   OL21 - 1968   OL22 - 1968

OL22 - 1975 - 90p   OL22 - 1981 - £1.80   OL23 - 1968   OL24 - 1969 - 10s. 6d.

OL24 - 1977 - £1.50   OL25 - 1969 - 12s. 6d.   OL26 - 1969

OL26 - 1992

OL27 - 1970   OL27 - 1980   OL28 - 1971 - 90p   OL28 - c.1975 - £1.35

OL28 - c.1980   OL29 - 1971 - £1.20   OL29 - 1983   OL29 - 1997

OL30 - 1972   OL31 - 1972   OL32 - 1972   OL32 - 2004

OL33 - 1971	OL33 - 2002	OL34 - 1973	OL34 - 1994
OL35 - 1973 - £1.60	OL35 - 1978 - £2.70	OL35A - 1973	OL35A - 1987
OL36 - 1973	OL37 - 1975	OL38 - 1975	OL39 - 1976
OL39 - 1991	OL40 - 1977	OL41 - 1977	OL42 - 1977

OL43 - 1977	OL44 - 1977 - £3	OL44 - c.1980 - £3.90	OL44 - 1994
OL45 - 1978	OL46 - 1978 - £2.40	OL46 - c.1980 - £2.70	OL46 - 2006
OL47 - 1979	OL48 - 1979	OL49 - 1979	OL50 - 1979
OL50 - 2007	OL51 - March 1936	OL51 - July 1936 - 2nd	OL51 - 1937 - 3rd

OL51 - 1949 - 4th - 6s.   OL51 - 1954 - 5th   OL51 - 1960 - 5th rp   OL51 - 1963 - 5th rp

OL51 - 1968   OL51 - 1972 - 6th - 90p   OL51 - 1977 - £1.35   OL51 - 1980 - £1.80

OL51 - 1983 - £2.40   OL51 - 1988 - 7th   OL51 - 1998   OL51 - 2005 - 8th

OL51A - 1936   OL52 - 1952   OL53 - 1953   OL53 - 1963

OL53 - c.1970   OL53 - 1978   OL54 - 1953   OL54 - 1963

OL54 - 1966 - 3rd   OL54 - 1974   OL54 - 1977 - 5th   OL54 - 1981 - £2.40

OL55 - 1954   OL55 - 1960   OL55 - 1965   OL55 - 1978 - 90p

OL55 - c.1980 - £1.35 OL55 - 1982   OL55 - 1992   OL56 - 1958

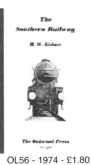

OL56 - 1970 - 18s./90p   OL56 - 1974 - £1.80   OL57 - 1962   OL57 - 1978

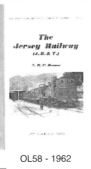

OL57 - 1983   OL58 - 1962   OL58 - 1969 - 18s.   OL58 - c.1970s - £1.35

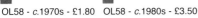
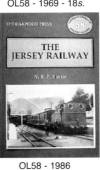

OL58 - c.1970s - £1.80   OL58 - c.1980s - £3.50   OL58 - 1986   OL58A - 1965

OL58A - 1973 - 90p   OL58A - 1977 - £1.15   OL58A - 1981 - £1.80   OL58A - 1986

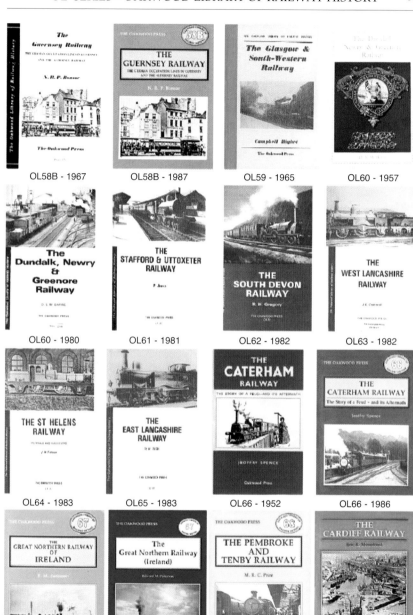

OL58B - 1967   OL58B - 1987   OL59 - 1965   OL60 - 1957

OL60 - 1980   OL61 - 1981   OL62 - 1982   OL63 - 1982

OL64 - 1983   OL65 - 1983   OL66 - 1952   OL66 - 1986

OL67 - 1986   OL67 - 2003   OL68 - 1986   OL69 - 1987

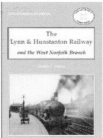

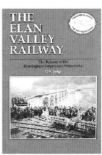

OL70 - 1987   OL70 - 2011   OL71 - 1987   OL71 - 1997

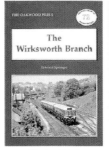

OL71 - 2004   OL72 - 1987   OL72 - 2004   OL73 - 1988

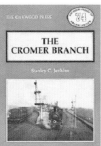

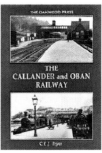

OL73 - 2011   OL74 - 1989   OL75 - 1989   OL76 - 1989

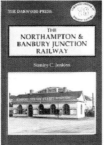
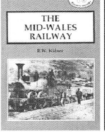
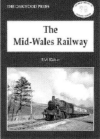

OL77 - 1989   OL78 - 1990   OL79 - 1990   OL79 - 2003

OL80 - 1991   OL80 - 2001   OL80 - 2004   OL81 - 1991

OL82 - 1991   OL83 - 1991   OL84 - 1992   OL85 - 1992

OL86 - 1993   OL86 - 2002   OL87 - 1993   OL88 - 1993

OL89 - 1993   OL90 - 1994   OL91 - 1994   OL92 - 1994

OL93 - 1995

OL94 - 1995

OL95 - 1995

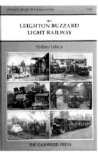

OL96 - 1996

OL97 - 1996

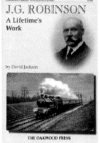

OL98 - 1996

OL99 - 1997

OL100 - 1998

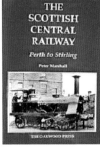

OL101 - 1998

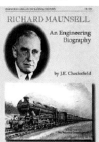

OL102 - 1998

OL102 - 2010

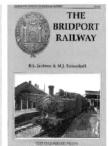

OL103 - 1998

OL104 - 1998

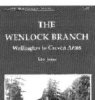

OL105 - 1998

OL106A - 1999

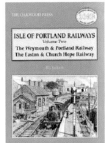

OL106B - 2000

 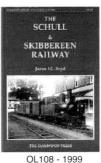 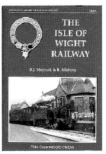

OL106C - 2000   OL107 - 1999   OL108 - 1999   OL109 - 1999

 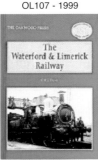  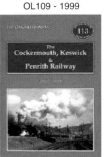

OL110 - 2000   OL111 - 2000   OL112 - 2000   OL113 - 2001

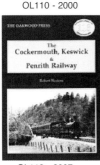 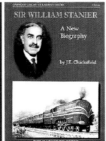 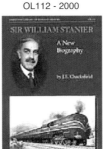 

OL113 - 2007   OL114 - 2001   OL114 - 2004   OL115 - 2001

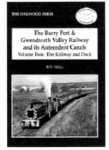 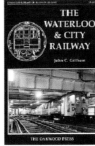 

OL116A - 2001   OL116B - 2009   OL117 - 2001   OL118 - 2001

OL118 - 2004

OL119 - 2001

OL120 - 2002

OL121 - 2002

OL122 - 2002

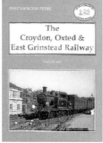

OL123 - 2003

OL124 - 2003

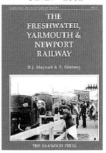

OL125 - 2003

OL126A - 2003

OL126B - 2003

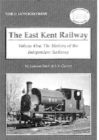

OL127A - 2003

OL127B - 2003

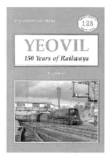

OL128 - 2003

OL129 - 2003

OL130 - 2004

OL131 - 2004

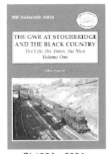
OL132A - 2004

OL132B - 2005

OL133 - 2005

OL134 - 2005

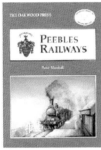
OL135 - 2005

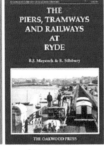
OL136 - 2005

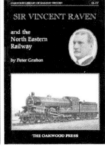
OL137 - 2005

OL138 - 2006

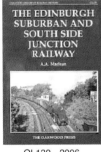
OL139 - 2006

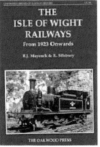
OL140 - 2006

OL141 - 2007

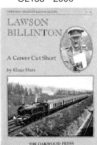
OL142 - 2007

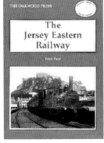
OL143 - 2007

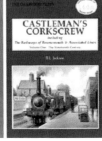
OL144A - 2007

OL144B - 2008

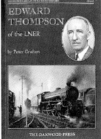
OL145 - 2007

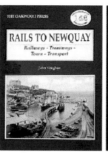
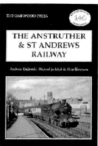

| OL146 - 2008 | OL147 - 2008 | OL148 - 2008 | OL149 - 2009 |

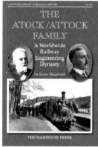
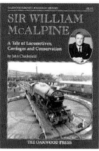
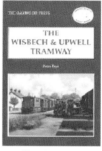

| OL150 - 2009 | OL151 - 2009 | OL152 - 2009 | OL153 - 2010 |

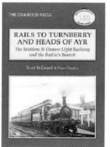

| OL154A - 2010 | OL154B - 2011 | OL155 - 2010 |

Section Eight

'PF' Series – Portfolios

This series was compiled by Mike Sharman to enable railway enthusiasts to collect most of the wide ranging drawings from the volumes of the *Locomotive* magazine. Each title consists solely of these fascinating fold out locomotive drawings to 7 mm scale.

Originally more titles were planned, as listed on the back cover of PF1, these have not been published. *Continental Railways Pre 1870; Great Western Railway Standard Gauge Part 2; Irish Railways; Great Eastern Railway Part 2; Railways of the World Miscellaneous; Great Northern Railway; London Brighton & South Coast Railway and the London, Chatham & Dover Railway; Stockton & Darlington Railway, The North Eastern Railway and Miscellaneous Locomotives; Scottish, Midlands Small Railways and the North London Railway;* plus volumes on wagons, coaches, etc.

PF1	*Broad Gauge of the GWR, Bristol & Exeter Railway, North and South Devon Railways*	M. Sharman
PF2	*London & North Western Railway*	M. Sharman
PF3	*Great Eastern Railway (Part 1)*	M. Sharman
PF4	*London & South Western Railway*	M. Sharman
PF5	*Great Western Railway 0-6-0 Standard Gauge Locomotives*	M. Sharman
PF6	*Boultons Sidings Including Contractors Locomotives*	M. Sharman

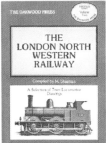

PF1 - 1985

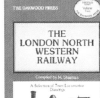

PF2 - 1986

PF3 - 1987

PF4 - 1989

PF5 - 1990

PF6 - 1989

Section Nine

'PS' Series – Portraits

A comparatively new Portrait series started in 1992 covering railway, tram and road transport, with the many varied pictures and expanded captions telling the story.

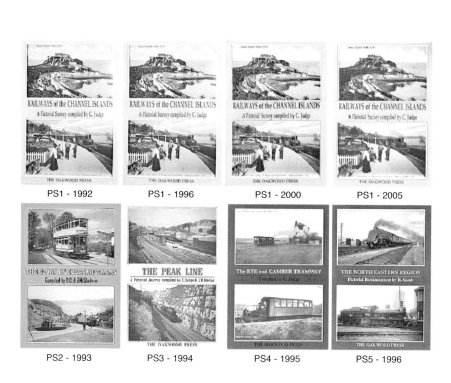

PS1 - 1992   PS1 - 1996   PS1 - 2000   PS1 - 2005

PS2 - 1993   PS3 - 1994   PS4 - 1995   PS5 - 1996

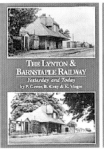

PS6 - 1997   PS7 - 1998   PS8 - 1999   PS8 - 2001

PS9 - 1999   PS10 - 2002   PS11 - 2003

Stockton Corporation double-decker, reproduced from *Aspects of Buses.*

Section Ten

'RS' Series – Reminiscences

Another new captivating series, featuring real life stories, mainly of railway life and the men who served the railways' needs. Most of the titles in this series are stories of careers on the railway from the 1940s onwards. One exception is 'LBSC' Footplate Experiences: Reminiscences at New Cross – experiences from around the turn of the 20th century. The two-volume Steel Wheels and Rubber Tyres covers a career that started on the railway before a switch to road transport.

Neil Fraser and Ruth Irons were historians who knew their subject intimately. Their books, Hillhouse Immortals and Woodford Halse respectively, captured the story of the communities in which they are set. In the case of Woodford Halse, S.C. Jenkins added further railway history.

Most James Boyd titles published by Oakwood appeared in the 'B' series (see page 16), Saga by Rail, his two volume account of his memories exploring some of the more obscure lines in the British Isles, was issued in the 'RS' series.

For those too young to have worked on the railway in the days of regular main line steam 'Over the Alps' tells of footplate work in the preservation era.

RS1	Cleaner to Controller, Reminiscences of the GWR at Taunton	W.J. Gardner
RS2	55 Years on the Footplate, Reminiscences of Southern at Bournemouth	S. Symes
RS3	Steaming Through War Years, Reminiscences on ex-GER Lines in London	R. Robertson
RS4	'LBSC' Footplate Experiences: Reminiscences at New Cross	L. Lawrence
RS5	Hillhouse Immortals: The Story of a LNWR Shed and its Men	N. Fraser
RS6	Woodford Halse: A Railway Community	R. Irons & S.C. Jenkins
RS7	Cleaner to Controller Vol. 2 Further Reminiscences of GWR at Taunton	W.J. Gardner
RS8	Through the Ranks on the Southern: A Career in the Nationalized Railway Industry	B.W. Aynsley
RS9	Dorset Footplateman, From Boyhood to Main Line Fireman	F. Andrews
RS10	Steel Wheels and Rubber Tyres Vol. 1 Transport around Oldham in the 1930s, Locomotives at Gorton in the 1940s and Leeds trams in the 1970s	G. Hilditch
RS11	Steel Wheels and Rubber Tyres Vol. 2 A General Manager's Journey: Manchester, Plymouth, Great Yarmouth, Halifax	G. Hilditch
RS12	From Steam to Stone, A BR Life - Engine Cleaner to Stone Projects Manager Vol. 1 - The Footplate Years	D. Butcher
RS13	From Steam to Stone, A BR Life - Engine Cleaner to Stone Projects Manager Vol. 2 - Onwards Into Management	D. Butcher
RS14	Testing Times at Derby - A Privileged View of Steam	A. Rimmer
RS15	On the Footplate at Bushbury 1947-1962: An Engineman's Tale	K. Terry
RS16	Saga By Rail: Ireland	J.I.C. Boyd
RS17	Saga By Rail: Great Britain and the Isle of Man	J.I.C. Boyd
RS18	Birmingham Footplateman - A Job for Life	D. Herbert
RS19	'Over the Alps' on the Watercress Line	J. Richardson
RS20	Neath Enginemen, Reminiscing Steam in South Wales	B. King
RS21	Dad had an Engine Shed, Some childhood railway reminiscences of a North Wales shedmaster's son	A.J. Robinson
RS22A	Under 10 CMEs Vol. 1 Dugald Drummond to W.A. Stanier 1912-1944	E.A. Langridge
RS22B	Under 10 CMEs Vol. 2 C.E. Fairburn to J.F. Harrison 1944-1959	E.A. Langridge
RS23	Steam, Diesels and On-Track Machines, from Colwick to Derby via the East Coast Main Line	J. Meredith

RS1 - 1994   RS2 - 1995   RS3 - 1996   RS4 - 1996

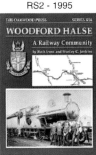

RS5 - 1999   RS6 - 1999   RS7 - 2000   RS8 - 2002

RS9 - 2003   RS10 - 2003   RS11 - 2004   RS12 - 2004

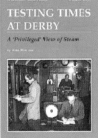
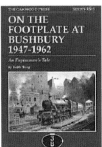

RS13 - 2004   RS14 - 2004   RS15 - 2006   RS16 - 2006

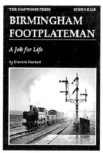

RS17 - 2007   RS18 - 2007   RS19 - 2008   RS20 - 2009

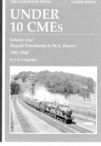

RS21 - 2010   RS22A - 2011   RS22B - 2011   RS23 - 2011

Section Eleven

'X' Series

A diverse mixture of around 100 interesting titles covering railway rolling stock, British and foreign railways, trams, ships, buses and aviation, as well as a few enjoyable non-transport titles. Some titles are a different size to the normal A5, also some of the earlier hardback titles were later reprinted in softback editions. X3 and X5 are subtitled 'The Railway Companion Series' and were meant to be read on the train by the railway traveller, telling the story of famous British main lines, from the earliest days to the then present; however, only these two railway companion titles were produced. A number of the out of print 'X' series can be quite difficult to find, but a few reprints and new titles appear quite regularly.

X1	*Great Northern Railway of Ireland* (NB: OL67)	E.M. Patterson
X2	*Giant's Causeway Tramway - Pioneer Hydro - Electric Railway*	J.H. McGuigan
X3	*Euston and Crewe Companion* (with 4 fold-out route sheets)	D.S.M. Barrie
X4	*North Devon & Cornwall Junction Light Railway*	D. Stuckey &
	(1980 edition not Oakwood)	C.F.D. Whetmath
X5	*Chester & Holyhead Railway Companion* (NB: OL25)	J.M. Dunn
X6	*South Eastern & Chatham Railway Locomotive List 1842-1952*	N. Wakeman
X7	*Twenty Four Inches Apart* (1981 edition not Oakwood)	S.M. Moir
X8	*London Independent Bus Album* (8 fold-out sheets of pictures)	R.W. Kidner
X9	*Locomotives of the Private Railways of Denmark*	W. Bay
X10	*First Hundred Road Motors*	R.W. Kidner
X11	*Rally Traction Engines*	A. Beaumont
X12	*Hundred Years of Road Rollers - A Pictorial Record*	Aveling Barford
X13	*Southern Region Chronology and Record 1803-1965*	R.H. Clark
X13A	*Appendix Southern Region Chronology and Record*	R.H. Clark
X14	*Hayling Billy: Life Story of the Engine Newington*	R.W. Kidner &
		R. Stent
X15	*Traction Engine Prints* (50 prints)	A. Beaumont
X16	*Namib Narrow-Gauge*	S.M. Moir &
		H.T. Crittenden
X17	*Traction Engines at Work*	H. Vizor
X18	*Edwardian Tramcars*	R.W. Kidner
X19	*Duffield Bank and Eaton Railways*	H. Clayton
X20	*Malta Railway*	B.L. Rigby
X21	*Leighton Buzzard Light Railway* (NB: OL96)	S.A. Leleux
X22	*Steam Over Belfast Lough*	R.M. Arnold
X23	*My Life in Steam*	K. Judkins
X24	*Miniature Railways Vol. 1 15 in. Gauge*	Clayton,
	(NB: Vol. 2 was to cover 7¼, 9½, and 10¼ in. lines and some 'oddities'	Butterell
	larger than 15 in., but was never printed)	& Jacot
X25	*Locomotives of the Danish State Railway*	W. Bay
X26	*Narrow Gauge Railway Museum*	J.I.C. Boyd
X27	*Commercial Vehicles of the World*	J.F.J. Kuipers
X28	*More of My Life in Steam*	K. Judkins
X29	*Index to Railway Model Drawings*	S.A. Leleux
X29A	*Index to Model Drawings: First Supplement 1973-4*	S.A. Leleux
X30	*Bagnalls of Stafford*	T.D.A. Civil &
		A.C. Baker
X31	*Malayan Railways Keretapi Tanah Melayu*	J.A. Stannistreet
X32	*Bygone Light Railways of Europe*	O.W. Laursen

X33	Model Boilers for Road and Ploughing Engines	J. Haining
X34	Carriage Stock of the South Eastern & Chatham Railway (NB: X52)	D. Gould
X35	Carriage Stock of the London, Brighton & South Coast Railway (NB: X54)	P.J. Newbury
X36	Reservoir Railways of Manchester and the Peak	H.D. Bowtell
X37	Maunsell's SR Steam Passenger (Carriage) Stock 1923-1939	D. Gould
X38	Register of GWR Absorbed Coaching Stock 1922/3	E.R. Mountford
X39	Reservoir Railways of the Yorkshire Pennines	H.D. Bowtell
X40	Bulleid's SR Steam Passenger Stock	D. Gould
X41	North Staffordshire Railway Locomotives and Rolling Stock	R.W. Rush
X42	Peak Line	J.M. Stephenson
X43	Private and Untimetabled Railway Stations, Halts and Stopping Places	G. Croughton, R.W. Kidner & P. Young
X44	Edwardian Postcards of Road and Rail Transport	D.E. Brewster
X45	London General Buses	D.E. Brewster
X46	Lancashire & Yorkshire Passenger Stock	R.W. Rush
X47	Barry Railway Diagrams and photographs of Locomotives, Coaches and Wagons	E.R. Mountford
X48	Vertical Boiler Locomotives and Railmotors Built in Great Britain	R.A.S. Abbott & J.W. Lowe
X49	Survey of Seaside Miniature Railways	D.J. Croft
X50	Southern Railway Passenger Vans	D. Gould
X51	Service Stock of the Southern Railway (NB: LP124)	R.W. Kidner
X52	Bogie Carriages of the South Eastern & Chatham Railway	D. Gould
X53	Locomotives and Rolling Stock of London, Tilbury & Southend Railway	R.W. Rush
X54	Bogie Carriages of the London, Brighton & South Coast Railway	D. Gould
X55	Lynton & Barnstaple Railway, An Anthology	D. Hudson & E. Leslie
X56	Great Northern Railway and East Coast Joint Stock Carriages from 1905	M. Harris
X57	Private Owner Wagons	B. Hudson
X58	Isle of Wight Here We Come, The Story of the Southern Railway's Isle of Wight Ships 1939-1945	H.J. Compton
X59	Isle of Wight Steam Passenger Rolling Stock	R. Maycock & M.J.E. Reed
X60	History of Slipping and Slip Carriages	C.E.J. Fryer
X61	Blackpool Trams, The First Half Century 1885-1932	P.H. Abell & I. McLoughlin
X62	Manifold Valley Railway, An Anthology	E. Leslie
X63	Encyclopaedia of Oxford Pubs, Inns and Taverns	D. Honey
X64	Ferry Services of the London, Brighton & South Coast Railway	S. Jordan
X65	Réseau Breton: A Rail Network in Brittany (2005 ed. with map X65M)	G. Gravett
X65M	Réseau Breton Railway Network fold-out map	
X66	Fifty Years of the West Sussex Fire Brigade 1948-1998	S. Jordan
X67	Railways of the Baie de Somme, A Landscape with Trains	Pacey, Arzul & Lenne
X67F	Les Chemins de Fer de la Baie de Somme, Le Réseau de Bains de Mer (French Text)	Pacey, Arzul, Lenne & Nickson
X68	Signal Boxes of the London & South Western Railway	G.A. Pryer
X69	Goodbye to Victoria, Story of Queen Victoria's Funeral Train	P.J. Keat
X70	Tramways a Vapeur du Tarn, A 60 cm Railway in South West France	S. Wright
X71	Quarry Hunslets of North Wales, The Great (Little) Survivors	C. Thomas
X72	Trams and Buses of Poole	C. Roberts & B.L. Jackson
X73	One Dog and his Man, A 2001 Farming Diary	K. Williams
X74	Cumbrian Railway Photographer, The William Nash Collection	K. Robinson & R. Forsythe
X75	Harrow & Wealdstone 50 Years On, Clearing up the Aftermath	P. Tatlow
X76	Weymouth to the Channel Islands, A Great Western Railway Shipping History	B.L. Jackson
X77	Radio Caroline, The Pirate Years	R.C. Humphries

X1 - 1962

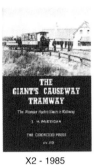

X2 - 1964

X2 - 1985

X3 - 1947

X4 - 1963

X5 - 1948

X6 - 1953

X7 - 1963

X8 - 1961 - 3s. 6d.

X8 - 196? - 5s.

X9 - 1959

X10 - 1950

X10 - c.1960s rp

X11 - 1965 - 9s. 6d.

X11 - 1973 - 2nd impression

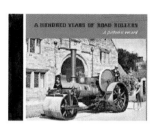

X12 - 1965   X13 - 1964   X13A - 1975

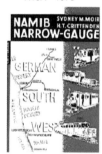

X14 - 1966   X15 - c.1966   X16 - c.1964

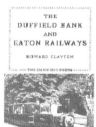

X17 - c.1966   X18 - 1968   X19 - 1968   X20 - 1970

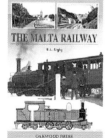

X20 - 2004   X21 - 1969   X22 - 1969   X23 - 1970

X23 - c.1972

X24 - 1971

X25 - 1961

X26 - 1972

X27 - 1972

X27 - 1972 (later?)

X28 - 1973

X29 - 1973

X29A - 1975

X30 - 1973

X31 - 1973

X32 - 1973

X33 - 1974

X34 - 1976

X35 - 1976

X36 - 1977

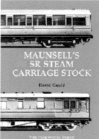

X37 - 1978 - £3   X37 - 1981   X37 - 1990   X37 - 2000

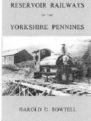

X38 - 1978   X39 - 1979   X40 - 1980   X40 - 1994

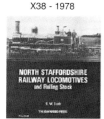

X41 - 1981   X42 - 1982   X43 - 1982   X44 - 1982

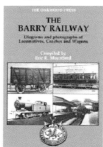

X45 - 1984   X46 - 1984   X47 - 1987   X47 - rear cover

X48 - 1989

X49 - 1992

X50 - 1992

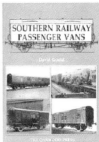

X50 - 1995

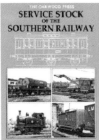

X51 - 1993

X52 - 1993

X53 - 1994

X54 - 1995

X55 - 1995

X56 - 1995

X57 - 1996

X58 - 1997

X59 - 1997

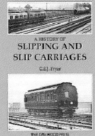

X60 - 1997

X61 - 1997

X62 - 1998

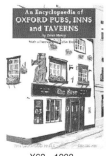

X63 - 1998   X64 - 1998   X65 - 1999   X65 - 2005

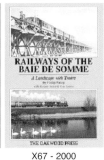

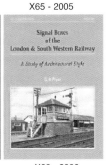

X66 - 1999   X67 - 2000   X67F - 2002   X68 - 2000

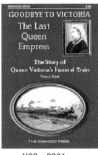

X69 - 2001   X70 - 2001   X71 - 2001   X71 - 2004

X72 - 2001   X73 - 2002   X74 - 2002

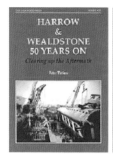 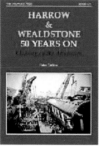 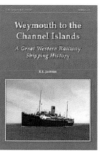 

X75 - 2002   X75 - 2008   X76 - 2002   X77 - 2003

X78 - 2004   X79 - 2005   X80 - 2005

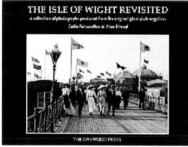 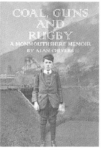 

X81 - 2005   X82 - 2005   X83 - 2006

  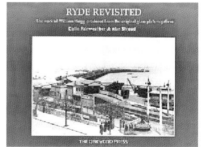

X84 - 2006   X85 - 2007   X86 - 2007

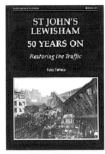  

X87 - 2007 X88 - 2007 X89 - 2008 X90 - 2008

X91 - 2008 X92 - 2008 X93 - 2009

  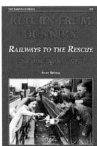 

X94 - 2009 X95 - 2009 X96 - 2010 X97 - 2010

 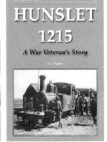 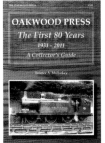

X98 - 2010 X99 - 2010 X100 - 2012

Alphabetical List

Notes: Titles in bold were in print at 31.12.2011. The items in the appendices on the following pages are not included in this alphabetical list.

Appendix One

'Z' Series –
Gramophone Records' Books

The 'Voices of the Past' titles mainly catalogue early sound recordings on gramophone records, from various record labels and countries, including spoken, documentary, orchestral, classical singers, violin, piano, opera and jazz. They list catalogue number, artist, title, composer, name of opera or other work, speed, matrix number, date of recording, label colour. The remaining titles also cover details on record collecting and information on the performers. (Oakwood did not use the 'Z' prefix, again used to aid identity.)

'Voices of the Past' titles
Z1	*Volume 1 HMV English Catalogue* (1978 ed. not Oakwood)	J.R. Bennett
	This volume was first published as six separate booklets	
	(5s .6d. each) comprising - main index; Part 1 Nos. 151 to 2-2733;	
	Part 2 Nos. 2-2735 to 3284; Part 3 Nos. 3285 to 04807,	
	Miscellaneous B298-B459; Part 4 Nos. B460 - B2098, C419 - C770;	
	Part 5 Nos. C772 - C1216, E3 - E398 D1 - D1024;	
	Complete Index. Parts 1- 5 paginated consecutively.	
Z2	*Volume 2 HMV Italian Catalogue*	J.R. Bennett
Z3	*Volume 3 Dischi Fonotipia* (1953 ed. not Oakwood, also 1969 ed.)	J.R. Bennett
Z3A	*Volume 3 Supplement to Dischi Fonotipia*	J.R. Bennett
Z4	*Volume 4 HMV International Red Label Catalogue 1*	J.R. Bennett, E. Hughes
Z5	*Volume 5 HMV Black Label Catalogue*	M. Smith
Z6	*Volume 6 HMV International Red Label Catalogue 2* (also 1970 ed.)	J.R.Bennett, E.Hughes
Z7	*Volume 7 HMV German Catalogue* (1978 ed. not Oakwood)	J.R. Bennett, W. Wimmer
Z8	*Volume 8 Columbia Catalogue English Celebrity Issues*	M. Smith
Z9	*Volume 9 HMV French Catalogue*	J.R. Bennett
Z10	*Volume 10 HMV Plum Label Catalogue*	M. Smith, F. Andrews
Z11	*Volume 11 HMV Russian Catalogue*	J.R. Bennett
Z12	*Label Discography of Long Playing Records: Columbia Series 1*	A.J. Poulton
Z13	*Label Discography of Long Playing Records: HMV Series 2*	A.J. Poulton
Z14	*Label Discography of Long Playing Records: HMV, Columbia Series 3*	A.J. Poulton

Other Gramophone Record Titles
Z15	*Record Collecting: A Guide for Beginners*	B. Semeonoff
Z16	*£-s-d of Record Collecting*	J. Martin
Z17	*Golden Age Recorded* (1946 ed. not Oakwood)	P.G. Hurst
Z18	*Archives of Sound*	J. Bescoby-Chamber
Z19	*John McCormack Discography* (1956 ed. not Oakwood)	L.F. MacDermott Roe
Z20	*Singers To Remember*	H. Simpson
Z21	*Smetana On 3000 Records*	J.R. Bennett

Z1 - *c.*1955 Main index   Z1 - *c.*1955 Part 1   Z1 - *c.*1955 Part 2   Z1 - *c.*1955 Part 3

Z1 - c.1956 Part 4   Z1 - c.1956 Part 5   Z1 - c.1956 36s.   Z1 - 1971

Z2 - 1957   Z2 - 1972   Z3 - 1964   Z3A - 1957

Z4 - 1961   Z4 - 1969   Z5 - 1961   Z5 - 1969

Z6 - 1961   Z7 - 1969   Z8 - 1970   Z9 - 1971

Z10 - 1974

Z11 - 1977

Z12 - 1975

Z13 - 1975

Z14 - 1975

Z15 - 1949

Z15 - 1951

Z16 - 1956

Z17 - 1963

Z18 - 1964

THE JOHN McCORMACK
DISCOGRAPHY

L. F. McDERMOTT ROE

Z19 - 1972

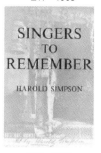

Z20 - 1972

Z21 - 1975

Appendix Two

'ZMR' Series – Market Research Books

These books were published by the Market Research Society in association with Oakwood Press. Specialist hardback titles, they were more than likely not published with any dust jackets. The contents were from various papers and essays with no single overall author. (Oakwood do not use the 'ZMR' prefix, again used to aid identity.)

ZMR1   *Readership Surveys - A Comparative Study* - 1954
        (this title may not have been published in association with Oakwood, but is part of the set)
ZMR2   *Statistical Sources for Market Research* - 1957
ZMR3   *Business Forecasting* by D. Pickard & others - 1958
ZMR4   *Attitude Scaling* - 1960
ZMR5   *A Bibliography of Papers Bearing on the Adequacy of Techniques Used in Survey Research*
        by W.A. Belson, C.R. Bell - 1960
ZMR6   *Marketing* - 1961
ZMR7   *Research in Advertising* - 1963
ZMR8   *New Developments in Research* - 1963
ZMR9   *Research in Marketing* by Rothman, Tate, Brown and others - 1964

ZMR2 - 1957   ZMR3 - 1958   ZMR4 - 1960   ZMR5 - 1960

ZMR6 - 1961   ZMR7 - 1963   ZMR9 - 1964

Railway Postcards

Railway Postcards published by the Oakwood Press, featuring some delightful early colour images of the Lynton & Barnstaple Railway. Oakwood advertised this set of four postcards for 60p in the February 1994 *Railway Magazine*. Each postcard has a reference on the back 'Series B No. 1, 2, 3 ,4' and they are based on the original *c*.1900 Peacock Series postcards published by the Pictorial Stationery Company, one of the earliest picture postcard publishers. The original Peacock Series were numbered between 2572-2585. The back cover of the *General Motor Bus Album* (A26) states: 'Photocards of buses and trams; List available', but I have not come across any of these.

B1 Lynton & Lynmouth Station   B2 - Chelfham Station

B3 Chelfham Viaduct and Station   B4 - Barnstaple Town Station

This attractive postcard was published by the Oakwood Press in the 1930s and is reproduced from a painting by J.E. Hoyland. The picture also appears on the front cover of some editions of *The Lynton & Barnstaple Railway* (OL51) by L.T. Catchpole, including the latest (2005) edition.

Appendix Four

Video and Audio Tapes

A natural follow-on to complement the 'Oakwood Library of Railway History', the Oakwood Video Library began producing videos in February 1993, maintaining the Oakwood tradition with top quality informative and entertaining productions. Titles soon extended to cover modern traction, steam archive, preservation, overseas, standard gauge and narrow gauge railways, while Oakwood Video Library also marketed other producers narrow gauge, bus and aviation titles, many of these having some level of Oakwood involvement during the production process. (*Note:* video and audio tapes illustrations are in the same order as the following lists.)

OVL Series – Oakwood Video Library – BR Steam Archive, British Narrow Gauge Archive
OVL1   *British Railways Steam 1967 - Steam's Swansong*
OVL2   *British Railways Steam 1968 - The End of an Era*
OVL3   *Manx Railways - Through the Years 1930s, 60s, 90s introducing the L.T. Catchpole Collection*
OVL4   *Railways of the North East in Retrospect*
         Ron Goult Collection Vol. 1 East Coast Main Line, Arteries, Freight, etc.
OVL5   *Lynton & Barnstaple Railway featuring the L.T. Catchpole Collection*
OVL6   *Railways of the North East in Retrospect*
         Ron Goult Collection Vol. 2 Cleveland and the Dales
OVL7   *LSWR Mainline, Vol. 1 Waterloo to Woking*
OVL8   *British Railways 1948-1994 From Nationalisation to Privatisation Vol. 1 - Goods to Railfreight*
OVL9   *British Railways 1948-1994 From Nationalisation to Privatisation Vol. 2 - Passengers to Customers*
OVL10   *Vale of Rheidol Light Railway - Through the Years featuring the L.T. Catchpole Collection*
OVL11   *LSWR Mainline, Vol. 2: Woking to Southampton*
OVL12   *Tallyllyn Railway through the Years featuring the L.T. Catchpole and P.B. Whitehouse collections*
OVL13   *Caledonian Routes, Vol. 1: Aberdeen, the Strathmore Line and Branches*
OVL14   *Southern Branch Lines & Byways Vol. 1: The Horsham to Guildford Direct Railway*
OVL15   *Caledonian Routes, Vol. 2: Perth to Glasgow and Stirlingshire Branches*
OVL16   *LSWR Mainline Vol. 3: Southampton to Bournemouth*
OVL17   *LSWR Mainline Vol. 4: Bournemouth to Weymouth*
OVL18   *Caledonian Routes, Vol. 3 Callander & Oban Line - Stirling to Crianlarich & the Killin Branch*

OVS Series – Oakwood Video Special – Preservation, British narrow gauge, overseas standard gauge and modern traction
OVS1   *Reunion of Steam 1968-1993, The fall and rise of British steam*
OVS2   *Steam in the Valley: Ten year history of the Keighley & Worth Valley Railway 1965-1975*
OVS3   *Manx Railway Centenarians, A Celebration*
OVS4   *The Story of the Groudle Glen Railway*
         encompassing memories of the Glen and Zoo in the heyday of Manx tourism (not issued)
OVS5   *Isle of Man Railways Steam 125, A Celebration*
         (produced in association with Isle of Man Railways)
OVS6   *Kosovo - A Train For Life: The greatest ever railway journey from Britain*

MT Series – Modern Traction Videos
MT1   *East Coast Resurgence - The Return of Royal Scots Grey* (in association with Deltic 9000 Locos Ltd)
MT2   *Unfinished Symphony Royal Scots Grey - The First Year*
         (in association with Deltic 9000 Locos Ltd)
MT3   *Destination Ramsgate* (in association with Deltic 9000 Locos Ltd)
MT4   *Perpetual Motion* (in association with Deltic 9000 Locos Ltd)
MT5   *The End of the '98 Cromptons - The Crompton Capitulation*
MT6   *VXC Weymouth*
MT7   *VXC Up Pompey! and other Solent wanderings*
MT8   *Riding the Pines Express from Manchester - last days of loco-hauled travel*
MT9   *Special Delivery - The 'Cornish Mails'*

TT Series Videos - Manx Cab rides
TT1   Travelling with the Motorman on the Manx Electric Railway
TT2   Travelling with the Motorman on the Snaefell Mountain Railway
TT3   Manx Combined Volume (TT1 and TT2 in double-video package)

WH Series Videos – West Highland Railway
WH100 West Highland Line - Official Centenary Video

OIE Series – Oakwood in Europe Videos
OIE1   La Vapeur Française - SNCF Archive from the Mike Grieves Collection
        (also available with French narration in PAL and SECAM)

Videos Distributed by the Oakwood Video Library
CV1   Tarrant Rushton - the Secret Airfield - 1942-1982 (Produced by Classic Video)
FF1   Concorde - In the 21st Century
        (produced by Fast Forward Productions with co-operation of British Airways)
FF2   Concorde - The New Era
        (produced by Fast Forward Productions with co-operation of British Airways)
FF3   Unused reference number.
FF4   Concorde - Around the World
        (produced by Fast Forward Productions with co-operation of British Airways)
FF5   Concorde - The Farewell
        (produced by Fast Forward Productions with co-operation of British Airways)
FF6   Farewell to the Routemaster
        (produced by Fast Forward Productions)
PB1   Puffing Billy, A Legend in Steam
        (produced by Greg Naylor, Tri-Media Services Australia)
WHR1   For the Love of Steam
        (produced by BECA Films)
WHR2   For the Love of Steam II - Reinstating the Welsh Highland Railway, Dinas-Waunfawr
        (produced by BECA Films)

OA Series – Oakwood audio stereo cassettes tapes
Diesel and steam sound effects with interesting information, giving great sound effects - something a
little different from Oakwood.

OA1   Sounds of 9000 - Reflections on Year One
        (produced in association with Deltic 9000 Locomotives Ltd)
OA2   Along West Highland Lines - An Insight into Two Classic Scottish Railways

OVL1 - 1993   OVL2 - 1993   OVL3 - 1993

OVL4 - 1993   OVL5 - 1993   OVL6 - 1994   OVL7 - 1994

OVL8 - 1994   OVL9 - 1994   OVL10 - 1994   OVL11 - 1994

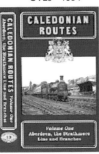
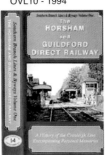

OVL12 - 1995   OVL13 - 1995   OVL14 - 1995   OVL15 - 1997

OVL16 - 1998

OVL17 - 2001

OVL18 - 2006

OVS1 - 1993

OVS2 - 1995

OVS3 - 1996

OVS5 - 1999

OVS6 - 2001

MT1 - 1997

MT2 - 1997

MT3 - 2000

MT4 - 2000

MT5 - 1999

MT6 - 2001

MT7 - 2003

MT8 - 2004

MT9 - 2004   TT1 - 1995   TT2 - 1995   WH100 - 1994

OIE1 - 1994   CV1 - 2000   FF1 - 2000   FF2 - 2001

FF4 - 2003   FF5 - 2004   FF6 - 2005   PB1 - 1992

WHR1 - 1998   WHR2 - 2000   OA1 - 1997   OA2 - c.2000

Appendix Five

DVDs

With the introduction of DVDs the Oakwood Video Library name was superseded by the new identity – 'Oakwood Visuals'. The programmes, once again, cover railways, with some other narrow gauge, aviation and bus DVDs also distributed, the Diagonal Entertainment brand being entirely in-house. The first Oakwood DVDs appeared in 2004 and now all new Oakwood programmes are being released on DVD. Some titles which originally appeared on VHS video are now also available in DVD format. Like the videos the DVDs continue to uphold Oakwood's tradition of top quality informative and entertaining viewing.

DE1DVD   *City of Truro - 102.3 - The return of a Great Western legend*
          (Diagonal Entertainment, distribution by Oakwood)
DE2DVD   *6024 - A Royal Progress - Lineside appreciation of King Edward I*
          (Diagonal Entertainment, distribution by Oakwood)
FF5DVD   *Concorde - The Farewell* (DVD version of FF5 video with extra coverage)
FF6DVD   *Farewell to the Routemaster* - as FF6 video with extra - The Double Decker - 1966
          (produced by Fast Forward Productions)
FF7DVD   *Routemaster - King of the Road* (Produced by Fast Forward Media)
FFDVD1   *Concorde 1976-2003 - 27 years of supersonic flight*
          (compendium of videos FF1/2/3 with extras - produced by Fast Forward)
FLOS1DVD *For the Love of Steam Vol. I - Re-instating the Welsh Highland Railway*
          (produced by Beca-TV, DVD version of WHR1 video)
FLOS2DVD *For the Love of Steam Vol. II - Re-instating the Welsh Highland Railway: Dinas- Waunfawr*
          (produced by Beca-TV, DVD version of WHR2 video)
FLOS3DVD *For the Love of Steam Vol. III - Re-instating the Welsh Highland Railway: Caernarvon-Rhyd Ddu*
          (produced by Beca-TV}
MT8DVD   *Riding the Pines Express from Manchester*
          (DVD version of MT8 video plus extra - Birmingham New Street to Coventry)
MT9DVD   *Special Delivery, The Cornish Mails*
          (DVD version of MT9 video plus extra - 'Arriving at Dawn' -
          through Truro to the Penzance buffer stops)
OVL13DVD *Caledonian Routes, Vol. 1 Aberdeen to Perth - The Strathmore Line and Branches*
          (DVD version of OVL13 Video)
OVL15DVD *Caledonian Routes, Vol. 2 Perth to Glasgow and Stirling Branches*
          (DVD version of OVL15 Video)
OVL18DVD *Caledonian Routes, Vol. 3 Callander & Oban Lines, Stirling to Crainlarich
          and the Killin Branch* (DVD version of OVL18 video)
OVL19DVD *Caledonian Routes, Vol. 4 Callander & Oban Line, Crianlarich to Oban
          and Ballachulish Branch*

DE1DVD - 2006

DE2DVD - 2007

FF5DVD - 2004

FF6DVD - 2005

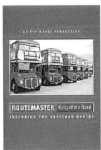

FF7DVD - 2006

FFDVD1 - 2004

FLOS1DVD - 2009

FLOS2DVD - 2009

FLOS3DVD - 2009

MT8DVD - 2004

MT9DVD - 2004

OVL13DVD - 2009

OVL15DVD - 2009

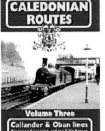

OVL18DVD - 2006

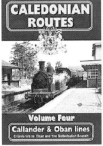

OVL19DVD - 2007

Appendix Six

Catalogues

The detailed Oakwood Catalogue was a relatively recent part of the Oakwood story being produced annually from 1988 to 2007 (with the exception of 1999 when Oakwood was moving from Oxford to Usk - just a winter 1998/99 price list was then published), prior to this leaflets had been used for information on titles. The catalogue evolved over the years, some of the early editions were only 150mm x 98mm in size, but the majority were 148mm x 210mm (A5), the same size as most of the Oakwood Press books. Pages also gradually increased from 24 to 36, and the black and white illustrations with single colour front cover progressed to full colour illustrations with glossy full colour covers. Starting in 1995 the catalogue also included extra unpaginated pages (growing from 4 to 8 pages), with full details on the Oakwood Videos and DVDs. The Oakwood catalogues offer a wealth of information on some book titles that are now out of print.

Today glossy detailed colour leaflets and price lists give full information on all current titles, with the Oakwood Press website www.oakwoodpress.co.uk, started in 2000, now taking on the task of regularly keeping everything fully up to date, with information on all current titles and lots more.

Interestingly, from 1998, the front cover of the catalogue featured London, Brighton & South Coast Railway 'E4' class 0-6-2 tank locomotive No. 488 *Oakwood*. This engine was built in 1899, and it survived into British Railways days ending its working days as No. 32488 (by then long unnamed). This also takes the story full circle as the original *Locomotion* magazine pictured the Stockton & Darlington Railway locomotive *Locomotion* on its front cover, which hauled the Stockton & Darlington's opening day train.

1988/1989   1989   1990   1991 - 60th Year   1992

1993   1994   1995   1996

1997	1998	1998/99 regional list	2000
2001 - 70 Years	2002	2003	2004
2005	2006	2007	
1930s leaflet	1980s leaflet	2010 flyer for OL154A	2010 list/order form

Appendix Seven

Collectors' Bookmarks

A card bookmark (186mm x 60mm) was supplied with each Oakwood Press book for a number of years starting in 1989, the latest being issued in 2007. The bookmarks are numbered, with an interesting picture on the front, in just one main colour at first, with some later black and white and full colour examples; on the back there is a selected list of Oakwood titles. No. 17 unusually features a poem entitled 'Trains'. They are collectable and some now sell for a few pounds.

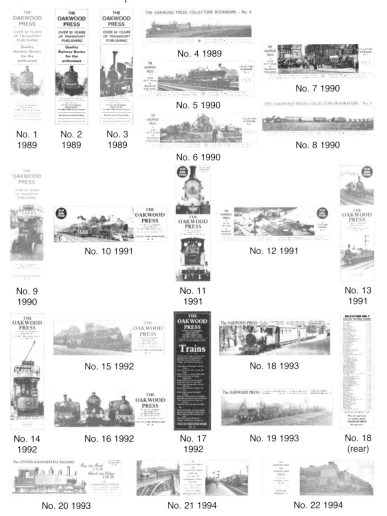

No. 4 1989

No. 7 1990

No. 5 1990

No. 8 1990

No. 6 1990

No. 1 1989

No. 2 1989

No. 3 1989

No. 10 1991

No. 12 1991

No. 9 1990

No. 11 1991

No. 13 1991

No. 15 1992

No. 18 1993

No. 14 1992

No. 16 1992

No. 17 1992

No. 19 1993

No. 18 (rear)

No. 20 1993

No. 21 1994

No. 22 1994

No. 23 1994   No. 24 1995   No. 25 1995

No. 26 1996   No. 27 1996   No. 28 1997

No. 29 1997   No. 31 1998

No. 32 1999   No. 30 1997 (front and back)   No. 33 2000

No. 34 2000   No. 35 2000   No. 36 2001

No. 37 2002   No. 38 2002   No. 39 2002

No. 40 2003   No. 41 2003   No. 42 2004

No. 43 2004   No. 44 2005   No. 45 2005

No. 46 2007

Appendix Eight

ISBN Numbers

The International Standard Book Number (ISBN) code is used to uniquely identify individual books and is issued to each new edition and revision of a book, but not straight reprints, they are also shown in the form of a bar code.

Early Oakwood titles do not have an ISBN code as Standard Book Numbering (SBN) codes were not introduced until 1966, when a nine digit code was created for each new book published. This continued to be used in the United Kingdom until 1974, when a 10 digit ISBN number was introduced. The ISBN code was first printed inside Oakwood Press books in 1979. From 1985 the ISBN code was also on the outside back cover and bar-coding was added to this in 1990.

Since 1st January, 2007 ISBNs have contained 13 digits and this latest code is the one used on the following pages. An example of the change is given for OL118 *Sir Nigel Gresley, An Engineer and his family* by Geoffrey Hughes. When first published in 2001 this book carried the number 0-85361-579-9, its 13 digit number became 978-0-85361-579-8. If you require the previous 10 digit ISBN codes the Oakwood Press website currently lists these in ISBN numerical order.

The ISBN 13 digit code is split into five distinct parts:

Part 1 - **978** - three digit code identifies the industry - denoting book publishing.
Part 2 - **0** - identifies the language-sharing country group (English).
Part 3 - **85361** - identifies the publisher - Oakwood's unique reference.
Part 4 - **579** - identifies the title - used also for reprints - new editions have new numbers.
Part 5 - **8** - Check digit - validates the ISBN - calculated (may vary on 10 digit).

The ISBN listing on the following pages is based on the official ISBN list (with only sections 4 and 5 shown), unfortunately this is incomplete in respect of some dates, particularly the earlier editions. Working out these has been very difficult and a great deal of time and effort has gone into trying to allocate correct dates, I am confident they are as accurate as possible with the information available.

Also there are some dates on the ISBN list that are different to those actually printed on the book, where this occurs the date in the book is used to help avoid confusion.

There were quite a number of other puzzles encountered; here are just a few examples: - ISBN codes started in 1966 yet some earlier titles such as X6 have an ISBN code. LP26 - the ISBN list shows the date as 1st January 1900 (over 50 titles have this date, I assume this is used where the date is not known) the actual publishing date was 1964 (this is, however, before the introduction of ISBN codes!). OL30 1972 has no code, LP227 and a few others have two different ISBN codes, OL1 - 1974 edition is not listed but other sources give this an ISBN code, PS1 - 1992 edition actually has two different ISBN codes printed on the book, the list goes on - I accept full responsibility for any errors that may still exist I have tried very hard to give complete accurate information, any updates are welcome.

The following pages list all Oakwood's books that have ISBN codes (using the latest 13 digit version), in Oakwood reference order A1A - Z21 , with the year published.

The index on pages 92 to 98 lists all titles ('Z' series pages 99 to 101) with the Oakwood reference. To further aid title identity by Oakwood reference, see Section One to Section Eleven.

Ref.	ISBN	Date	Ref.	ISBN	Date	Ref.	ISBN	Date
A1A	077 9	1965	LP20	038 0	1963	LP55	337 4	1987
A3	037 3	1964	LP20	269 8	1980	LP56	100 4	1972
A4A	062 5	1965	LP21	069 4	1963	LP56	334 3	1987
A7	060 1	1967	LP21	447 0	1995	LP56	516 3	1999
A24	216 2	1978	LP22	084 7	1963	LP57	104 2	c.1972
A31	039 7	1964	LP22	338 1	1986	LP58	103 5	1972
A32	* 020 2	1999	LP22	509 5	1997	LP59	107 3	1972
* Prefix 978-0-95370			LP23	075 5	1964	LP60	112 7	1972
			LP23	318 3	1985	LP60	541 5	1999
B1A	080 9	1965	LP24	063 2	1964	LP61	111 0	1972
B1A	167 7	1975	LP25	058 8	1964	LP62	109 7	1972
B1B	081 6	1962	LP25	388 6	1990	LP63	110 3	1972
B1B	168 4	1975	LP26	043 4	1964	LP64	124 0	1973
B2	082 3	1967	LP27	067 0	1964	LP65	127 1	1973
B2	133 2	1973	LP28	070 0	1964	LP65	320 6	1985
B2A	444 9	1993	LP28	189 9	1975	LP66	126 4	1973
B2B	469 2	1994	LP28	252 0	1978	LP67	128 8	1973
B2C	479 1	1996	LP28	382 4	1989	LP68	130 1	1973
B3A	024 3	1970	LP29	096 0	1964	LP68	372 5	1988
B4A	115 8	1972	LP30	068 7	1965	LP68	557 6	2000
B4A	365 7	1988	LP30	350 3	1987	LP69	119 6	1973
B4B	383 1	1989	LP32	091 5	1964	LP69	324 4	1986
B5A	273 5	1981	LP33	093 9	1967	LP70	131 8	1973
B5B	312 1	1985	LP33	376 3	1989	LP70	370 1	1990
B5C	328 2	1986	LP34	090 8	1966	LP71	146 2	1973
			LP35	053 3	1967	LP71	431 9	1993
C1A	041 0	1967	LP35	229 2	1978	LP72	147 9	1974
C1B	042 7	1968	LP36	079 3	1967	LP72	515 6	1999
C1C	009 0	1969	LP36	335 0	1988	LP73	150 9	1974
C2	143 1	1971	LP37	197 4	1976	LP73	333 6	1987
C2	332 9	1986	LP37	233 9	1978	LP74	148 6	1974
C2	562 0	2000	LP38	095 3	1968	LP75	149 3	1974
C3	154 7	1975	LP38	378 7	1989	LP76	153 0	1974
C3	412 8	1991	LP39	221 6	1968	LP77	152 3	1974
C4	220 9	1977	LP39	407 4	1992	LP78	157 8	1974
C5	261 2	1980	LP40	002 1	1968	LP79	156 1	1974
C6	398 5	1990	LP40	342 8	1986	LP80	161 5	1974
C7	404 3	1990	LP41	001 4	1968	LP81	163 9	1974
C8	468 5	1994	LP42	004 5	1968	LP81	487 6	1996
C9	490 6	1996	LP43	006 9	1968	LP82	159 2	1975
C10	563 7	2000	LP43	336 7	1987	LP83	164 6	1975
			LP44	010 6	1969	LP84	160 8	1975
LP3	056 4	c.1967	LP45	013 7	1969	LP85	162 2	1975
LP5	051 9	1968	LP45	351 0	1987	LP86	171 4	1975
LP5	182 0	1975	LP46	018 2	1970	LP86	316 9	1985
LP5	052 6	c.1966	LP46	413 5	1991	LP87	170 7	1975
LP7	172 1	1976	LP47	017 5	1970	LP88	169 1	1975
LP7	433 3	1992	LP48	092 2	1970	LP89	180 6	1976
LP7	040 3	c.1966	LP48	230 8	1978	LP90	181 3	1976
LP9	086 1	1961	LP49	094 6	1970	LP91	184 4	1976
LP10	072 4	c.1967	LP49	405 0	1993	LP91	317 6	1990
LP10	319 0	1985	LP50	097 7	1970	LP92	186 8	1976
LP11	031 1	1966	LP50	381 7	1988	LP92	436 4	1995
LP14	048 9	1961	LP51	021 2	1971	LP93	187 5	1976
LP15	047 2	1961	LP52	022 9	1971	LP94	183 7	1976
LP17	071 7	1962	LP52	392 3	1992	LP95	185 1	1976
LP18	035 9	1962	LP53	144 8	1971	LP96	190 5	1976
LP18	422 7	1991	LP54	102 8	1972	LP97	193 6	1976
LP19	245 2	1979	LP55	101 1	1972	LP98	192 9	1976

Ref.	ISBN	Date	Ref.	ISBN	Date	Ref.	ISBN	Date
LP99	199 8	1976	LP150	348 0	1987	LP202	510 1	1997
LP100	205 6	1976	LP151	307 7	1984	LP203	430 2	1997
LP101	198 1	1976	LP152	308 4	1984	LP204	505 7	1997
LP102	191 2	1977	LP153	309 1	1984	LP205	518 7	1997
LP103	201 8	1977	LP154	310 7	1985	LP206	528 6	1998
LP104	213 1	1977	LP155	311 4	1985	LP206	715 0	2011
LP105	210 0	1977	LP156	321 3	1985	LP207	504 0	1998
LP106	208 7	1977	LP157	323 7	1986	LP208	523 1	1998
LP107	217 9	1977	LP158	326 8	1986	LP209	530 9	1998
LP108	224 7	1978	LP159	340 4	1986	LP209	665 8	2007
LP109	227 8	1978	LP160	313 8	1986	LP210	531 6	1998
LP110	237 7	1978	LP161	346 6	1986	LP211	539 2	1999
LP111	239 1	1978	LP161	556 9	2000	LP212	546 0	1999
LP111	368 8	1988	LP162	354 1	1987	LP213	553 8	1999
LP112	240 7	1978	LP163	352 7	1987	LP213	662 7	2007
LP113	241 4	1978	LP163	646 7	2005	LP214	559 0	2000
LP113	415 9	1992	LP164	356 5	1987	LP215	558 3	2000
LP114	246 9	1978	LP165	358 9	1987	LP216	560 6	2000
LP115	247 6	1979	LP166	359 6	1988	LP217	567 5	2000
LP116	249 0	1979	LP167	367 1	1988	LP218	578 1	2001
LP117	243 8	1979	LP168	373 2	1988	LP219	585 9	2002
LP118	251 3	1979	LP169	379 4	1988	LP220	582 8	2002
LP119	253 7	1979	LP170	380 0	1989	LP220	692 4	2009
LP120	257 5	1979	LP171	369 5	1989	LP221	584 2	2002
LP121	259 9	1980	LP172	393 0	1989	LP222	588 0	2002
LP121	371 8	1988	LP173	389 3	1989	LP223	594 1	2002
LP122	255 1	1980	LP174	391 6	1990	LP224	620 7	2004
LP123	256 8	1980	LP175	394 7	1990	LP225	622 1	2004
LP124	263 6	1980	LP176	395 4	1990	LP226	617 7	2004
LP125	262 9	1980	LP177	399 2	1990	LP227	600 9	2004
LP126	266 7	1980	LP177	675 7	2008	LP228	639 9	2005
LP127	267 4	1980	LP178	411 1	1990	LP229	641 2	2005
LP128	265 0	1980	LP179	414 2	1991	LP230	650 4	2006
LP129	264 3	1981	LP180	420 3	1991	LP231	652 8	2006
LP130	271 1	1981	LP181	419 7	1991	LP232	667 2	2007
LP131	270 4	1981	LP182	425 8	1992	LP233	678 8	2008
LP132	274 2	1981	LP183	426 5	1992	LP234A	703 7	2010
LP132	403 6	1990	LP183	634 4	2005	LP234B	704 4	2011
LP133	279 7	1981	LP184	424 1	1992	LP234C	705 1	2011
LP134	278 0	1981	LP184	711 2	2011	LP235	708 2	2010
LP135	280 3	1981	LP185	440 1	1993			
LP136	272 8	1982	LP186	438 8	1993	MS0	341 1	1986
LP137	283 4	1982	LP187	450 0	1993	MS1	*670 6	1983
LP138	289 6	1982	LP187	668 9	2007	MS2	*671 3	1982
LP139	285 8	1982	LP188	448 7	1994	MS2A	501 9	1996
LP140	291 9	1983	LP189	475 3	1995	MS3	*673 7	1984
LP141	284 1	1983	LP190	464 7	1995	MS4	421 0	1991
LP142	293 3	1983	LP191	480 7	1995	* Prefix 978-0-95090		
LP143	296 4	1983	LP191	714 3	2011			
LP143	375 6	1988	LP192	481 4	1996	OL1	074 8	1967
LP143	471 5	1995	LP193	483 8	1996	OL1	204 9	1974
LP143	655 9	2006	LP194	488 3	1996	OL2	027 4	c.197?
LP144	299 5	1983	LP195	499 9	1996	OL3	065 6	c.1971
LP145	300 8	1983	LP196	495 1	1996	OL5	085 4	c.196?
LP146	301 5	1984	LP197	502 6	1996	OL5	231 5	1978
LP147	298 8	1984	LP198	494 4	1996	OL6	028 1	1966
LP148	297 1	1984	LP199	493 7	1997	OL6	234 6	1978
LP149	304 6	1984	LP200	512 5	1997	OL8	215 5	1977
LP150	303 9	1984	LP201	486 9	1997	OL9	026 7	1973

Ref.	ISBN	Date	Ref.	ISBN	Date	Ref.	ISBN	Date
OL9	463 0	1995	OL53	232 2	1978	OL97	482 1	1996
OL10	036 6	c.1968	OL54	073 1	1966	OL98	497 5	1996
OL10	214 8	1977	OL55	049 6	1965	OL99	513 2	1997
OL11	360 2	1987	OL55	439 5	1992	OL100	527 9	1998
OL12	361 9	1988	OL56	055 7	1970	OL101	522 4	1998
OL13	087 8	1973	OL57	025 0	1962	OL102	526 2	1998
OL13	410 4	1991	OL57	236 0	1978	OL102	695 5	2010
OL16	076 2	c.197?	OL58	030 4	1969	OL103	520 0	1998
OL16	402 9	1990	OL58	344 2	1986	OL104	533 0	1998
OL17	045 8	1961	OL58A	029 8	1965	OL105	500 2	1998
OL18	088 5	1965	OL58A	345 9	1986	OL106A	540 8	1999
OL19	302 2	1984	OL58B	145 5	1967	OL106B	551 4	2000
OL20	268 1	1967	OL58B	329 9	1987	OL106C	566 8	2000
OL21	000 7	1968	OL59	044 1	1965	OL107	532 3	1999
OL22	005 2	1968	OL60	260 5	1980	OL108	534 7	1999
OL22	174 5	1975	OL61	277 3	1981	OL109	544 6	1999
OL23	007 6	1968	OL62	286 5	1982	OL110	550 7	2000
OL24	012 0	1969	OL63	288 9	1982	OL111	543 9	2000
OL25	008 3	1969	OL64	292 6	1983	OL112	545 3	2000
OL26	015 1	1969	OL65	295 7	1983	OL113	564 4	2001
OL26	435 7	1992	OL66	325 1	1986	OL114	576 7	2001
OL27	089 2	1970	OL67	343 5	1986	OL115	573 6	2001
OL28	023 6	1971	OL67	602 3	2003	OL116A	577 4	2001
OL29	223 0	1971	OL68	327 5	1986	OL116B	685 6	2009
OL29	491 3	1997	OL69	347 3	1987	OL117	525 5	2001
OL31	099 1	1972	OL70	330 5	1987	OL118	579 8	2001
OL32	105 9	1972	OL70	713 6	2011	OL119	580 4	2001
OL32	626 9	2004	OL71	353 4	1987	OL120	583 5	2002
OL33	108 0	1971	OL71	517 0	2004	OL121	586 6	2002
OL33	595 8	2002	OL72	349 7	1987	OL122	589 7	2002
OL34	116 5	1973	OL72	625 2	2004	OL123	598 9	2003
OL34	454 8	1994	OL73	374 9	1988	OL124	605 4	2003
OL35	117 2	1973	OL73	712 9	2011	OL125	601 6	2003
OL35A	118 9	1973	OL74	384 8	1989	OL126A	604 7	2003
OL35A	362 6	1987	OL75	387 9	1989	OL126B	610 8	2003
OL36	129 5	1973	OL76	377 0	1989	OL127A	608 5	2003
OL37	176 9	1975	OL77	366 4	1989	OL127B	609 2	2003
OL38	175 2	1975	OL78	390 9	1990	OL128	612 2	2003
OL39	194 3	1976	OL79	406 7	1990	OL129	613 9	2003
OL39	409 8	1991	OL79	606 1	2003	OL130	618 4	2004
OL40	203 2	1977	OL80	400 5	1991	OL131	629 0	2004
OL41	200 1	1977	OL80	574 3	2001	OL132A	627 6	2004
OL42	212 4	1977	OL81	408 1	1991	OL132B	630 6	2005
OL43	209 4	1977	OL82	416 6	1991	OL133	632 0	2005
OL44	218 6	1977	OL83	417 3	1991	OL134	633 7	2005
OL44	458 6	1994	OL84	423 4	1992	OL135	638 2	2005
OL45	219 3	1978	OL85	427 2	1992	OL136	636 8	2005
OL46	238 4	1978	OL86	437 1	1993	OL137	640 5	2005
OL46	653 5	2006	OL86	587 3	2002	OL138	644 3	2006
OL47	248 3	1979	OL87	443 2	1993	OL139	645 0	2006
OL48	250 6	1979	OL88	442 5	1993	OL140	656 6	2006
OL49	225 4	1979	OL89	452 4	1993	OL141	657 3	2007
OL50	244 5	1979	OL90	456 2	1994	OL142	661 0	2007
OL50	658 0	2007	OL91	457 9	1994	OL143	664 1	2007
OL51	032 8	c.1968	OL92	441 8	1994	OL144A	666 5	2007
OL51	123 3	1971	OL93	478 4	1995	OL144B	686 3	2008
OL51	363 3	1988	OL94	476 0	1995	OL145	672 6	2007
OL51	637 5	2005	OL95	474 6	1995	OL146	673 3	2008
OL53	054 0	1963	OL96	460 9	1996	OL147	676 4	2008

Ref.	ISBN	Date
OL148	677 1	2008
OL149	687 0	2009
OL150	681 8	2009
OL151	688 7	2009
OL152	689 4	2009
OL153	696 2	2010
OL154A	700 6	2010
OL154B	717 4	2011
OL155	699 3	2010
PF1	314 5	1985
PF2	315 2	1986
PF3	331 2	1987
PF4	386 2	1989
PF5	396 1	1990
PF6	397 8	1989
PS1	432 6	1992
PS1	434 0	2005
PS2	453 1	1993
PS3	465 4	1994
PS4	473 9	1995
PS5	489 0	1996
PS6	508 8	1997
PS7	496 8	1998
PS8	537 8	1999
PS9	511 8	1999
PS10	581 1	2002
PS11	607 8	2003
RS1	445 6	1994
RS2	484 5	1995
RS3	472 2	1996
RS4	498 2	1996
RS5	548 4	1999
RS6	529 3	1999
RS7	568 2	2000
RS8	597 2	2002
RS9	615 3	2003
RS10	614 6	2003
RS11	616 0	2004
RS12	623 8	2004
RS13	624 5	2004
RS14	628 3	2004
RS15	649 8	2006
RS16	651 1	2006
RS17	663 4	2007
RS18	670 2	2007
RS19	683 2	2008
RS20	691 7	2009
RS21	707 5	2010
RS22A	701 3	2011
RS22B	716 7	2011
RS23	718 1	2011
X1	066 3	1962
X2	057 1	1964
X2	294 0	1983
X6	078 6	1953

Ref.	ISBN	Date
X7	061 8	1963
X10	050 2	c.196?
X11	222 3	1965
X12	064 9	1965
X13	033 5	1964
X18	003 8	1968
X19	034 2	1968
X20	016 8	1970
X20	621 4	2004
X21	011 3	1969
X22	014 4	1969
X23	019 9	1970
X24	020 5	1971
X27	114 1	1972
X28	120 2	1973
X29	125 7	1973
X29A	173 8	1975
X30	165 3	1973
X31	132 5	1973
X32	122 6	1973
X33	151 6	1974
X34	196 7	1976
X35	195 0	1976
X36	207 0	1977
X37	228 5	1978
X37	401 2	1990
X37	555 2	2000
X38	235 3	1978
X39	242 1	1979
X40	258 2	1980
X40	467 8	1994
X41	275 9	1981
X42	282 7	1982
X43	281 0	1982
X44	290 2	1982
X45	305 3	1984
X46	306 0	1984
X47	355 8	1987
X48	385 5	1989
X49	418 0	1992
X50	428 9	1992
X51	429 6	1993
X52	455 5	1993
X53	466 1	1994
X54	470 8	1995
X55	485 2	1995
X56	477 7	1995
X57	492 0	1996
X58	506 4	1997
X59	507 1	1997
X60	514 9	1997
X61	503 3	1997
X62	519 4	1998
X63	535 4	1998
X64	521 7	1998
X65	536 1	1999
X66	549 1	1999
X67	554 5	2000
X67F	590 3	2002

Ref.	ISBN	Date
X68	565 1	2000
X69	569 9	2001
X70	570 5	2001
X71	575 0	2001
X72	572 9	2001
X73	591 0	2002
X74	592 7	2002
X75	593 4	2002
X75	680 1	2008
X76	596 5	2002
X77	611 5	2003
X78	619 1	2004
X79	631 3	2005
X80	635 1	2005
X81	642 9	2005
X82	643 6	2005
X83	648 1	2006
X84	647 4	2006
X85	659 7	2007
X86	660 3	2007
X87	669 6	2007
X88	671 9	2007
X89	674 0	2008
X90	679 5	2008
X91	684 9	2008
X92	682 5	2008
X93	690 0	2009
X94	693 1	2009
X95	694 8	2009
X96	697 9	2010
X97	698 6	2010
X98	702 0	2010
X99	709 9	2010
X100	719 8	2012
Z1	134 9	1971
Z2	135 6	1972
Z3	136 3	1969
Z4	137 0	1969
Z5	141 7	1969
Z6	138 7	1970
Z7	139 4	1969
Z8	142 4	1970
Z9	140 0	1971
Z10	166 0	1974
Z11	206 3	1977
Z12	177 6	1975
Z13	178 3	1975
Z14	179 0	1975
Z16	059 5	1956
Z17	046 5	1963
Z18	098 4	1964
Z19	106 6	1972
Z20	113 4	1972
Z21	158 5	1975

Appendix Nine

Oakwood People

Early Days

Co-founder of the Oakwood Press, Roger Wakely Kidner, was born in Sidcup, Kent on 16th March, 1914. He passed away on 14th September, 2007 aged 93, then living near Aberystwyth. Beryl Kidner (née Walton) married Roger in 1943 and assisted him in running the business, she passed away in 1995. Roger also worked in Fleet Street as a reporter and sub-editor and in publishing for Benn Brothers, later in advertising, before making Oakwood Press his full time occupation.

Co-founder of the Oakwood Press Michael J. Robbins was born in London on 7th September, 1915 and he passed away on 21st December, 2002. From 1939 to 1980 his main job was with London Transport. Oakwood Press was never his full time occupation and his involvement was only in the earlier years, although he remained firm friends with Roger Kidner.

Latter Years

The current Oakwood team is very much a family affair led by proprietor Jane Kennedy. Daughter, Julie Lewis, is office manager, her husband, John, is the warehouse manager. Son Ian is the book designer and Chris Potts the editor. Son Andrew produces the DVDs with his wife, Della, and long time friend and colleague Roger Smith.

The Authors

To complete the story a mention should also be made of all the Oakwood Press authors, who have contributed so much time and effort into recording a remarkable amount of transport history for posterity.

Many of the authors are well-known and involved with multiple titles, whilst others have just written a single title, using their own specialized knowledge. Without all their efforts none of these books could have been published.

Oakwood Press takes this opportunity to thank every single one of them.

Most of the Oakwood team are seen in this photograph. *From left to right:* Andrew, John, Julie, Jane, Della and Ian. *Author*